The Geek's Guide to the Writing Life

An Instructional Memoir for Prose Writers

Stephanie Vanderslice

Bloomsbury Academic
An imprint of Bloomsbury Publishing Plc

B L O O M S B U R Y
LONDON · OXFORD · NEW YORK · NEW DELHI · SYDNEY

Bloomsbury Academic

An imprint of Bloomsbury Publishing Plc

50 Bedford Square	1385 Broadway
London	New York
WC1B 3DP	NY 10018
UK	USA

www.bloomsbury.com

BLOOMSBURY and the Diana logo are trademarks of Bloomsbury Publishing Plc

First published 2018

© Stephanie Vanderslice, 2018

British Library Cataloguing-in-Publication Data
A catalogue record for this book is available from the British Library.

ISBN:	HB:	978-1-3500-2356-7
	PB:	978-1-3500-2355-0
	ePDF:	978-1-3500-2358-1
	eBook:	978-1-3500-2357-4

Library of Congress Cataloging-in-Publication Data
Names: Vanderslice, Stephanie, author.
Title: The geek's guide to the writing life : an instructional memoir for prose writers / Stephanie Vanderslice.
Description : London; New York : Bloomsbury Academic, 2017. | Includes bibliographical references and index.
Identifiers: LCCN 2017010087| ISBN 9781350023567 (hb) | ISBN 9781350023550 (pb)
Subjects: LCSH : Authorship. | Creation (Literary, artistic, etc.) |

Classifi... ...ecord

To find out ... ...bury.com.
Here yo... ...oming

Contents

Acknowledgments

This book is dedicated to writing geeks but it would not exist without editors, specifically the editorial team at Bloomsbury, including David Avital, Lucy Brown, Lisa Carden, and Mark Richardson, whose vision and insight have proved instrumental at every step along the way, from conception to production to publication.

For their support and encouragement, I wish to thank my family—it is often said that everyone needs a champion in their youth and I am fortunate to have had several, including my parents, Maureen Pettei and William Muller, and my mother-in-law, Patricia Vanderslice. In addition, I remain indebted to the friends and mentors and writing geeks who have shared my journey, especially: Margot and Ralph Treitel, Hannah Treitel Cosdon, Blanche Boyd, Richard Bausch, Alan Cheuse, Mary Ann Wilson, Kevin McCann, Chris Motto, William Lychack, and Anna Leahy, as well as my writing group members, Donna Wake and Jeff Whittingham. It is also important to mention that this book would not exist without the generous nature of my childhood friend, Jay Kirsch, who helped me get started on the *Huffington Post*. Finally, I wish to thank my students, who enrich my life in so many ways it is impossible to imagine it without them.

Most of all I am grateful to my husband, the *real* John Vanderslice and our own little realm of writing-geek love. It has made all the difference.

Introduction: The geeks and the cool kids

I have always been the opposite of cool. In literary society, a place generally inhabited by people blinking out from behind Buddy Holly glasses (with or without lenses) and kicking around in their wing tips or Doc Martens, this makes me something of an outsider. A geek. Not the kind of geek who can quote lengthy passages from *Star Wars*, although I have given birth to people with this talent. No, I mean that, literally or metaphorically, I've never sat at the cool kids' table in the cafeteria—whether in high school or in the literary world—in my life. I wouldn't even know what to do or say there if I had. I'm ok with this reality. In fact, I'm kind of proud of it. In fact, I think most people share this reality with me. Face it, the cool kids' table just isn't that big.

Just as there are cool and uncool people in high school, freaks and geeks, brains and jocks, name your stereotype, there are also cool writers and uncool writers. Some of this might have to do with talent (Ann Patchett, for example, is cool in my opinion, because she is such a luminous writer), some with drive (Elizabeth Gilbert, famous as she might be right now, faithfully waited tables for over a decade while she wrote), some with talent *and* drive. Come to think of it, both Gilbert and Patchett are not only talented but also waited tables. And Patchett should get extra points for doing so at TGI Fridays, where she had to wear suspenders and be cheerful all the time. Some of it might have to do with trends (Do you have tattoos? Yes? One coolness point for you!), attitude, good fortune, and the ability to hold one's liquor. Some of it also has to do with early success, loosely defined as achieving a high profile in the literary world before the age of forty, and publishing a lot of books while pulling down a lot of grants and awards and residencies along the way. This is all well and good. I'm a great champion of literary culture, even if it means I must endure yet another feature story about the "friendly" competition between two bespectacled, bearded authors for "voice of his generation" bragging rights (pronoun deliberate; they don't call them pissing contests for nothing).

But what if you are not in this category and you still feel driven to write, you've always felt driven to write, to create, yes even to publish, to share your work with someone else?

This book is for you. I'm calling it a prose writer's memoir because as a terminally unhip writer, an outsider who has nonetheless managed to lead a pretty fulfilling writing life, I think what I've learned so far and the stories of how I learned it can be useful for the rest of us, for those who did not go to Iowa or Yaddo or grab an NEA grant or a Guggenheim along the way.

Do I sound bitter? I don't mean to, because I'm not bitter, actually. The fact is, I never applied to Iowa or Yaddo or tried to get an NEA grant (having gotten my MFA back in the day, when *Poets and Writers* magazine was still printed on black and white newsprint and professional development was something business people, not artists, did, I didn't even know those last two were things you were *supposed* to aim for, like steps on a ladder). George Mason University, where I got my degree, was always my first choice and I got in to all three programs where I applied. Anyway, even if I had achieved some of those distinctions, I still probably wouldn't be cool. What with all this genome mapping, it's only a matter of time before they discover that there's actually a gene for coolness. Don't waste the gene splicer. I can tell you right now: I don't have it.

But here's the thing—you don't really have to be cool to be a writer. Even the terminally unhip like me can do it. Lean in here and I'll tell you the secret, something you'll read over and over again in this book: Leading a writing life is more about *doing the writing* than anything else. Doing the writing when no one else really cares what you're doing, because—lean back in, I wasn't finished—*they don't*. It's also about figuring out a way to make space for that writing in your life and then, maybe finding some success with it, however you define that. Because even though most writers would still write even if they were the last person on earth, publishing a few things, maybe even a book, here and there, proof that we are still connecting with others through our words, is sometimes the extra little push we need to keep us going.

In fact, the more I think about my definition of writing geek and weigh what's "hip" and what is not, the more I think that geeks like us might be especially suited for the writing life *because* of our enthusiasm for it. Stay with me here. The word "geek" is a synonym for the word "nerd." Stratospherically gifted young adult author John Green defines being a nerd like this:

> .... nerds like us are allowed to be unironically enthusiastic about stuff ... Nerds are allowed to love stuff, like jump-up-and-down-in-the-chair-can't-control-yourself love it when ... people call people nerds, mostly what they're saying is, "you like stuff." Which is just not a good insult at all. Like, you are too enthusiastic about the miracle of human consciousness.[1]

In this context, being a writing geek is something to be proud of. In a world of sound bites and people who roll their eyes at blocks of text longer than a paragraph, we're the people who have lists of "favorite words," people who gasp audibly or stare off in the distance at a particularly breathtaking line. Maybe we mortify friends and family with our lack of irony and ability to control our enthusiasm, but that's ok. As literature ebbs and flows in the twenty-first century and threatens to morph into something else entirely, I'd certainly rather be on the side of celebrating it rather than regarding the miracle of language with cynicism and disdain.

But that does not mean that people like us don't get a little discouraged sometimes, that we don't wonder how we're going to keep all that jumping-up-and-down-in-the-chair intensity burning, to find the time to get it from our heads to the page, when the world doesn't really want us to. When we're tired from our day job and our friend from college just published a book or bought a McMansion at 24 on her pharmacist's salary (be honest, you don't really want a McMansion anyway, you just want to be able to afford one) and you just don't know how to scrape up the energy and the motivation to keep writing when the rewards seem few or are, let's face it, nonexistent.

This book is here, *I am here,* to help you.

When I look back over my last thirty years and settle my gaze upon the naive, dewy eighteen-year-old writing geek I once was, I can't believe I'm still here, doing this, that I still get to do this (although I'm telling you now, you do not need anyone's permission), that I even get paid to teach writing to young people. While I am tempted to say how lucky I am, because that's what everyone seems to say about life in the arts, really, luck did not have that much to do with it. Whether I was mindful of them or not—honestly, I think I became more mindful as the years progressed—a lot of the steps I took to become the successful writing geek I am today were fairly deliberate. As a result, I feel certain that while the writers at the cool table may be few, if you read this guide and follow my lead, the satisfying life of a writing outsider is well within your grasp.

If you don't believe me, now is a good time to tell you about one of my mentors in writing geekery, Margot Treitel.

Margot Treitel was my best friend, Hannah's, mother. When I met her, in 1989, I was graduating from college and standing on the cusp of a writing life. For graduation, Margot, a widely published poet, gave me a copy of her chapbook, *The Inside Story,* which contained poems about her early years in the Peace Corps in West Africa, about family life, about growing older. I did not know then that chapbook or book-giving is symbolic for poets—a sign of respect—but I did feel validated. How I wish she and her husband, Ralph, had lived long enough that I could have returned the favor with one of my own books.

Well known in the Maryland literary arts scene and beyond, Margot and Ralph Treitel founded the *Little Patuxent Review* in Columbia, Maryland, in the 1970s as a way to build the arts scene in the Mid-Atlantic—and build it they did, with readings, festivals, public access T V shows. In fact, the *Review* was revived ten years ago in their memory and I have even had the honor of being rejected from it (they haven't seen the last of me yet).

Ralph and Margot lived in a townhouse in Columbia, Maryland, and until Ralph's debilitating stroke, he held a day job with the Social Security Administration while Margot raised their daughters and continued to write, publish, and perform her work in hundreds of venues. Their lives were modest in style but rich, so rich, in art. Books and videos (they were also movie buffs) lined the walls, African art mixed with a Victorian settee.

Since I was pursuing my MFA in writing only an hour and a half away, Hannah and I often used her parents' home as a central meeting place. So while I witnessed one kind of writing life when someone like Robert Stone or Tim O'Brien blew into town via my MFA program, holding court for a few hours at a bar like the Tiki Lounge in

Washington, D.C., the lessons I learned at Ralph and Margot's home were more powerful and lasting.

Author Carol Lloyd, whose book, *Creating a Life Worth Living: A Practical Course in Career Design for Artists, Innovators and Others Aspiring to a Creative Life*, I recommend highly for anyone considering a literary life (published in 1997, it is telling that it remains in print), points out that we have a rather black and white, either/or way of viewing success in the arts in America. Either we achieve success on the level of Stephen King or Amy Tan, that is, making a flush living purely through our art, or we are abject failures, mopping the orange tile floors at Burger King. This fatalistic attitude eliminates the gray area, the in-between, where it is possible to pursue art and make a living, although they are not always the same thing. But the gray area—for an artist, a writer, the gray area is everything.

One of my writing mentors, Richard Bausch, used to remind us to cherish the relationships we were forming in our MFA program because once we returned to the "outside world," we would once more find ourselves among the masses of people for whom writing and reading, *words*, didn't mean as much as they did to us (always a people pleaser, I took his advice so far as to marry one of my classmates). He was right about this, of course. Just like music conservatories and art schools, writing programs are one way for generations of writers to find and support one another. Margot and Ralph were another way. When I was with them, I felt as if I had found some of my "people," (it helped, of course, that their daughter was my best friend, and as a dancer and actress, her artistic nature was one of the many qualities that drew me to her). Here were people who lived and breathed the literary arts and also raised families without starving. People who didn't think a standard career—medicine, finance, law—was the only professional aspiration worth having. Margot, especially, lived in that gray area, in the in-between, and she showed me that it was possible.

Everyone who wants a career in writing or the arts should have a Margot Treitel in their lives. That's what I'm trying to do with this book. Be your Margot Treitel.

Margot and Ralph weren't the only ones. There was also my father, who pursued his passion for photography in the 1970s right out of a career teaching community college English and right into founding the college's first photography course and, over time, an entire photography and digital media department. People who showed me that if you keep swinging away at that piñata, especially from different angles and vantage points, eventually some candy is going to fall out. But here's the thing: It's not even about the candy; it's about the swinging; you've got to like the process of swinging away.

By modeling the different kinds of artistic lives that could be led in the "gray" area, these people made the life I live today, an incredibly rewarding—if a little frantic—one possible. Over the years, I've tried to do the same thing for my students and I want this book to do the same thing for you.

Let me pause here to tell you a bit about my students, because in a way, this book is sort of a love letter to them as much as it's a love letter to you and to the nascent writer I once was.

As a group, my students love words and stories just as much as I do. In fact, right now I have the good fortune of teaching the Harry Potter generation, the generation that made reading trendy again, the generation that has steeped itself in the tea of seven-hundred-page books with the heft of a VCR. Coming, as they do, from the heart of the mid-South, however, which still lags behind the rest of the U.S. in the percentage of college graduates, they are, more often than not, first-generation college students.

What you need to know about first-generation college students is that they have often been raised in families that fought hard for every rung of the economic ladder they have ascended and for whom the rung below them and the rungs after that have always been perilously close. Families like these cotton to the idea of their children becoming writers or artists about as much as they do to the idea of them becoming pole dancers, the latter of which might at least seem to offer more financial security. Families like these have no idea how or even whether to encourage their budding scribes; families like these did not scrimp and sacrifice to bring their children to the doorstep of higher education only to have them choose a path that *seems* to guarantee them nothing but financial insecurity. In fact, in order to understand where families of these students are coming from, now might be a good time to mentally revisit the "Stephen King vs Burger King floor-mopper" analogy. To these families, I might as well be dealing as much in meth as in words for all the good I am doing their children.

And my students *are* other people's children, the living, breathing vessels of their hopes and dreams. I take my responsibilities for these young (mostly) adults pretty seriously, just as I do my responsibilities toward you in writing this book. I have no intention of leading my students or you down a primrose path paved with generous royalty checks. At the same time, I have no intention of telling them (or you) that the writer's life is reserved for a precious few elect and that the rest of us ought to memorize the phrase, "I owe, I owe, it's off to work I go," so that we can apply it to our bumpers or copy it into our Facebook statuses in recognition that we've accepted our grim fate.

After all, you would do the same thing if you were in my place, or, at least, I like to think you would. If you taught young women like Camille, who filled boxes of notebooks with imaginary worlds and once recounted how, when she was little and got going telling one of her "stories," from the backseat of the family car, her father learned that the best course of action was to pass their destination and just keep driving. Or like Evan, whose stories, each quirkier than the next, mystified his passively supportive family, which only compelled him to write more of them, to render the world as he alone saw it. Or, finally, like Melissa, who was rejected from graduate writing programs for two years running but who kept working and writing until she found the one that recognized her gifts, around the same time that she began to publish and win awards for her work.

Finally, when I think about encouraging someone to pursue a writing life, I think of the scene in one of my favorite movies, *Moonstruck*, when Cher's character, Loretta, has just confessed her affair with her fiancé's estranged younger brother, Ronny Cammareri (Nicolas Cage), to her beleaguered mother, Rose (Olympia Dukakis).

Rose: "Do you love him, Loretta?"[2]
Loretta: "Aw, ma. I love him awful."
Rose: "Oh, God, that's too bad."

Obviously, I do not think a life driven by the desire to write is necessarily a terrible thing, or I would have given it up a long time ago. And Rose does not necessarily want her daughter to live a life untouched by true love. What's important here is the recognition that neither kind of life is easy. What matters is what this book is here to tell you, from one writing geek to another: That it's possible. The only person who knows if you have what it takes is the only person who matters. You.

On having what it takes

It happens at least once a semester. A student writes me an impassioned note (often an email) begging me to tell her whether she has what it takes to be a writer, imploring me to "stop her right now," if she doesn't. I've been teaching for over twenty years and I have yet to completely figure out what, exactly, this student is asking for, or why they're asking for it. If they are simply asking for permission to keep writing, that's a no-brainer. As I've said before, the only person who should be deciding whether you bring words into being is you.

But here's why they're asking for permission. Because they've had to ask for it their whole lives—that is, even when they didn't ask for it, there was probably someone out there who was trying to prevent them from taking the risk to try their hand at some kind of art. Let me explain.

Americans are big on gatekeeping. Our society thrives on the extent to which people are allowed or not allowed to do something. We worry that the more people who are allowed to do something, the less precious it is. Seriously, this keeps some of us up at night—the idea that too many people want to express themselves when everyone "knows" that only a limited number of people get through that gate. Because we like to fetishize our "Artists," we set up an especially large number of gates to protect them and their preciousness. Few people, it seems, are actually allowed to become artists, but lots of people, from grade school teachers on up, appoint themselves the arbitrators, the people who get to decide who those precious few are. I myself have plenty of other things to lose sleep over, like creating my own art in the midst of an otherwise hectic life.

A couple of examples: I lead a course for future teachers on teaching creative writing and invariably students on this course ask me what I should do if one of their students is not "talented." How should they "tell" that student? The range of students asking this question is impossibly wide. Some plan to teach elementary school, some high school, some college. Regardless, this is a matter of great concern to each of them. Who gets "anointed"? Who is allowed to continue on this path of becoming that most precious of all things, an artist, and how do we let the non-elect down easy?

Stop and think about this for a moment. What gives these students, these future teachers, who aren't even necessarily writers or even readers themselves, the right to judge a fourth grader, a ninth grader or a first-year college student, people who are all in vastly different developmental stages as writers, and the right to decide if they should be encouraged to continue. What gives anyone that right?

Close your eyes. Picture the student who has always aspired to teach fourth grade taking aside nine-year-old Grace, who scribbles in her notebook every chance she gets, and telling her that, in his opinion, her metaphors lack a certain *je ne sais quoi* and that instead of wasting her time writing in that notebook, she'd better work on her ability to make change. Can you see it? Good.

Now, imagine the young man who has just discovered James Baldwin in tenth-grade poetry. He has never written a word before but suddenly he's inspired to write page upon page imitating his new favorite poet. His work is that of a beginner—*because he is one*—but he's discovered a deep well inside himself. But my student, as his teacher, feels compelled to tell him that while that's all well and good, it might be better to leave the poetry to the "real" poets.

Finally, I want you to imagine me, or someone similarly endowed with the power to make or break a nineteen-year-old's dreams, reading one of the first efforts of one of my creative writing students—let's call her Emily—and deciding that, nope, this just does not have that certain spark I was expecting to see right out of the gate.

Dear Emily,

You ask if you have what it takes to be a writer? Based on the one assignment you've turned in, I have to admit, you're no Joyce Carol Oates or Toni Morrison. The good news is, I hear there's still room in that Accounting class.

Here is the truth: If I only taught the students who immediately presented themselves as possessing that mysterious, "What it takes," (whatever that is—the fact that different people get to define it in different ways ought to give us all pause), I would be standing in front of an empty classroom because there wouldn't be anyone to teach. In fact, the front of the classroom itself might be pretty empty because for every teacher over the years who "anointed" me for my writing gifts, there was another who didn't think I was anything special—and did not hesitate to let me know it. In other words, for every Mr McCann, who announced in the middle of AP World Literature one day, "Stephanie Muller is the best writer in this school," there was Mrs Anderson, who strode over to Kristen McKenzie and me, the only two students who had come to her review session for the AP Composition test, clapped Heather on the shoulder and said, "I'm counting on you, Heather. You are my 5." (For those who have never had a high-school student in their lives, this is the highest score you can get.)

My heart sank. I should note, here, that I was passionate about writing in high school and my grades in the class until that point reflected those passions. The year before I had scored a 99 on the statewide regents exam in the subject. But for whatever reason, as a student, I was not Mrs Anderson's cup of tea.

But I turned out to be her 5, too. And yes, I am obviously still bitter about the whole thing, but I like to think that soul-crushing experience made me a better teacher. I try not to play favorites, but what's more, I never count anyone out. People can surprise you. I love surprises.

Another couple of stories, just to show that I'm not the only teacher who prefers to withhold judgment on a writer's ability to "make it." Many years ago, I was a student of late fiction writer and NPR book critic Alan Cheuse. At the bar after class one night, a few of us pressed him to tell us which of his students had "made it," as writers. He hemmed and hawed, took a sip from the glass of red wine he habitually nursed through these affairs and finally offered a few names we recognized. "The thing is," he emphasized, "it's not always the ones you predict."

A few years later, while interviewing a well-known author with many years of experience who was a candidate for a position at my university, one of the members of the hiring committee asked if he had ever told a student to give up on a writing career for lack of talent or if he could ever imagine a future circumstance in which he would deliver this kind of news.

Well-known author sat up and looked at us, a little dumbfounded. "Why no, I never have and I don't think I ever would," he said. "To be honest, it's simply too hard to tell."

Back to the student begging me to tell her if she has what it takes to make it or if she should "stop writing right now." The best I can do is to tell her that it's not up to me. It's up to her. Is she willing to keep reading and practicing writing until her pens run dry or the letters wear off her keyboard? Because that is what she needs to be doing right now in her embryonic career. Is she willing to keep writing even when no one else is reading her work, even if no one else cares whether she writes or not? Because all that matters, really, is that she cares. And is she willing to keep writing even after an editor, agent, or anonymous colleague has just delivered a withering critique of her work, the kind that stops less determined people cold?

The truth is, having been at this writing thing for all of my adult life, I can tell you that many of my peers, some more talented than me (and if you stay with writing long enough, people who are more talented than you are a dime a dozen) simply stopped writing along the way. There is nothing wrong with that. If you don't feel compelled to write, if you don't feel you must write, that you cannot go very long without a narrative or a poem or an essay—name the genre—taking shape in your head and then working its way out—then don't. It's not about having the time or the talent—it's about having the compulsion—and the determination.

All right. Enough with the preaching, for now. I don't know about you, but I can only read about the philosophy of the writing life in the abstract for so long before I want to trap the author by the lapel and say, "Yes, yes, this is all good but tell me what to do!"

And I *love* writing life books. Not the "write your novel in a year on Friday nights because there's nothing good on TV anyway," books (aka, how-to-write books, although these can have their place) but writing life books, where one particular author sheds some light on how she does it. So it makes sense that I would eventually write one. But I encourage you to seek them out. Sure, it's possible to overdose on them, just like anything else, but to my mind, writing life books are kind of like pep talks; we all need them once in a while to remind us of the difficulty and the importance of what we're trying to do. In fact, we need a collection of them, so we can just pull one off the shelf at will when we're feeling particularly low. There's a list of them at the end of this book, but my favorite writing life authors are Anne Lamott, Elizabeth Gilbert, Heather Sellers, and Robin Black. You can't go wrong with any of them. You really can't.

Back to, "I want to know how to put all this lofty philosophy into practice, I want to know more about what to do to *make* a writing life." That's what the rest of this book is going to do. Fortunately, you can start right now. Read on for a preview:

Chapter 1—Making the commitment

If the title of this chapter sounds a little like committing to an exercise program, that's because committing to a writing life is not unlike choosing to exercise and stay fit. You need to make certain overarching lifestyle changes to support it, like trying to start a new habit. Committing to a writing life happens in different ways for different writers. I'll tell you how it happened for me and what I learned and also include some cautionary tales. Chapter 1 focuses on the big picture issues of this commitment: Work choices, partner choices, family choices, financial choices, and what to do when some of those choices don't work out.

Chapter 2—Doing the work (and, sometimes, not doing the work)

If Chapter 1 focused on how to commit to a writing life in the "big picture" sense of the word, Chapter 2 focuses on the nitty-gritty, day-to-day stuff. How do you make the time for this kind of work? How do you maximize that time? How do you fit your family and friends and all the other stuff of life into a twenty-four-hour day? What do you do about writer's block? What do you do about sleep? All of these issues amount to defending your time to write in a world that really does not want you to do it. No offense, world, it's not personal; we simply live in a state of relentless overstimulation and hyper-connection and this state is not conducive to the solitude and reflection a writer needs. Don't worry, though, I have developed a number of adaptations that get me through this. Here I offer them to you as well. Learn from my experience—and my mistakes.

Chapter 3—Connecting with readers: Publishing

It is true that writers are people who need to make sense of the world through words and who would do this whether or not these words were published. But let's be honest, at a certain point most of us also want to connect with readers. There's nothing wrong with this impulse and as long as you're not counting on your publishing success to pay your rent, realizing this desire to connect is not always as hard as some might make it look. Connecting happens gradually, in baby steps. There are a lot of resources for this online and in print, resources I'll share in the Appendix, but I've developed some effective practices of my own over the years. Think of this chapter as a narrative of my own publishing journey and a blueprint to help you map out your own.

Chapter 4—Writing geeks unite: Finding your tribe

Although most writers, including myself, crave solitude, when you choose to write, you are also identifying yourself as part of a literary community, a community that can come in handy in an era of crowd-sourcing and collaboration. Claiming a space for yourself in your own generation and your own literary community is also important in sustaining yourself as a writer. This kind of work can be hard and lonely; you need your people more than ever. You also need them to make your way in an increasingly interconnected world in which yes, networks are important. Chapter 4 focuses on how to find these people and keep them close, how to make sure you are giving back to the literature community as much as it gives to you.

Chapter 5—Continuing your education: What makes sense for you?

Master's degrees, Master's of Fine Arts degrees, Doctoral degrees, writing conferences, online courses, face-to-face workshops. You'd think this romantic endeavor called writing was teachable or something. It should come as no surprise to you by this point that I think creative writing can be taught. In fact, I have even published books with that title and could bore you for pages with my own ideas about why people keep beating this dead horse every so often, as if no one ever though of it before (hint: Questioning the teachability of creative writing seems to be a kind of shorthand for one of two things. 1. I am one hip curmudgeon; or 2. I was traumatized by a creative writing program at some point in my life and have never gotten over it). When I say "teachable," I simply mean that there are lots of ways to learn to be a better writer. These methods are not one-size-fits-all, however. For some people, a Master's of Fine Arts degree (MFA) is the way to go, for others, a Ph.D. is the ultimate goal, especially if they hope to teach. But for others, community writing courses, writing conferences, and a healthy dose of autodidacticism constitute the best route. This chapter will help you decide which educational paths will be best for you.

Chapter 6—Making a living: Careers that support the writing life

Once upon a time, F. Scott Fitzgerald could take some time off from novel writing (what he considered a more serious task) and conjure up a few short stories for the *Saturday Evening Post* to keep him, and Zelda, solvent. Those days are long over. It has become more and more difficult for writers to support themselves full-time at all with their writing, but especially when they're just starting out. Many writers have day jobs: Poets Ted Kooser and Wallace Stevens were insurance executives, Elizabeth Berg was a nurse, Toni Morrison was an editor, and many writers teach college, like me. This chapter will examine the kinds of jobs that best support a developing writing career —those aligned with the arts and those that are not—and help you decide what might best support yours.

Chapter 7—Being teachable

So I've been at this writing life thing unofficially since I was six years old and officially since I was eighteen, which gives me a nice span of years to reflect on, a lot of friends who have come and gone, as well as hundreds of writing students. While I would never tell someone they don't have "what it takes," I do know that the friends, colleagues, and students I've had over the years who are *still writing* have one trait in common. It's not talent. It's not even persistence, though that is the other essential trait for a writer. No, what these friends, colleagues, and students have in common is that they were *teachable*. Rather than pontificating, they were quietly paying attention, absorbing whatever they could from those around them, from teachers, peers, books. Instead of talking, they were listening, always looking for and open to what the world had to teach them. This chapter will explore the research that explains the importance of "teachability" in a writer, and how you can cultivate this teachability in yourself.

Chapter 8—Writing 2.0 or, platform-building can be fun

There was a time in the not so distant past when to be a writer, all you needed to do was read, write, and publish (granted, getting past the gatekeepers in publishing has never been easy). For those writers who gained their status then and retain it now, that may still be the case. For the rest of us, those days are also over. The good news is that if you're mindful about it, you can build an organic platform that represents just another dimension of who you are as a person and as a writer, a platform that becomes part of your work rather than siphoning energy from it. Building a platform is also an essential part of being a good literary citizen, of becoming interested in the careers, work, and processes of other writers and artists, of the community around you. This chapter will show you how to start doing that.

Chapter 9—Traditional book publishing today: Finding and working with an agent

Writers who write prose often end up writing books and seeking representation, or a literary agent, for those books. Student writers and writers in the community often tell me that they are mystified by this process, frequently asking my advice. The truth is, it's no mystery if you know how to go about it. Using examples from my own successful agent search and others, Chapter 9 will show you the best methods for finding an agent, as well as what doesn't work.

Chapter 10—Making the show: They said "No." Now what? Or, they said "Yes!" Now what?

In the classic 1988 movie *Bull Durham*, about a minor league baseball team in Durham, North Carolina, players often dreamed about making the "show," or being called up from the minor leagues to play for a major league team. The literary equivalent is having your book published by a major publisher—one of the big five houses or a major independent. This chapter will give you the lowdown on the "show" or the traditional publishing world, describing the different kinds of publishing houses and different kinds of publishing options, including publishing with smaller independent publishers. Again, drawing on my own experience and those of colleagues, this chapter will include how to recalibrate and press on if your work is turned down by these houses and what to expect if your work is accepted.

Chapter 11—Non-traditional book publishing: What you need to know

With the rise of e-books and publishing-on-demand, non-traditional publishing, including self-publishing, has become a central part of the ever-shifting publishing landscape. This chapter will look at some of the models that work and some of the reasons why a writer might want to pursue them, and will also detail some less-savory options that writers will want to avoid.

Chapter 12—Before you go: Why we do this

Chapter 12 will offer parting words on the reasons why we write, reasons that aren't really connected to publishing at all but to our actual practice, to the process itself and to having something to say and saying it. Here, we'll come full circle and remind ourselves why we're writing geeks in the first place, and how that, in and of itself, is a gift.

Appendix

The Appendix of this book will be chock-full of places for you to expand on what you've learned here. It will include a list of what I consider to be top books out there for writing support and inspiration, as well as books about the field and a number of descriptive lists of websites and online writing communities to support your writing life and help you publish your work. Bloomsbury, the publishers of this book, and I will also keep these resources up to date with a website intended to become another port of call for you where these resources will not only be updated and added to and where you can follow my tweets.

Before we head off

Before we begin this journey together, let me say a few more words about writing life books in general and this one on particular. As I've said, I've read a lot of writing life books and to my mind, any book worth its salt is going to present one particular view, one very specific, biographic, if you will, perspective, on the writer's life. As a result, this book is going to be pretty opinionated, full of my own unambiguous ideas about how the writer's life worked for me and about how you might learn (or not) from my example. Some of these ideas may resonate deeply with you—that is my goal, for my favorite part of a writing life book is when I read a sentence that makes my heart sing, "Yes! I feel that way too!" or, "That doesn't just happen to me?" And then, if I'm lucky, I even learn a solution to a writerly problem I have— but at the very least, I have someone to commiserate with across the page-time continuum.

But some of these ideas may not resonate with you. And that's okay too. That doesn't mean you should follow them anyway or that you should just stop reading—it means that some of the ideas I have as a writer may not work for you. Others might. Keep going.

I am going out of my way to explain this because I have found, in my work with new writers over the years, that they tend to fall along a spectrum when it comes to writing advice, from following every single thing the latest craft book or author tells them, regardless of whether it really helps them, to not only rejecting another writer's advice but actually getting angry about it. Angry as in, for example: "This chapter says she writes all her first drafts by hand and that she suggests her students do the same. She goes on and on about writing by hand. I hate writing by hand. Is this author going to tell me what to do for the rest of this book?" Then, a few chapters later, if the same author is still giving examples of what works for them, the same writers are still complaining, "Why does she keep telling us what to do?"

As an aside, we live in a funny cultural moment—many writers are hyper-sensitive to the slightest whiff that we are being "told what to do." Yet, many of these same writers still insist on a very rough, severe kind of writing critique: "tell it like it is—don't sugarcoat it—I can take it!" that suggests that when it comes to critiquing writing, conscious, constructive comments that require the reviewer to simply engage in a little diplomacy and emotional intelligence are quaint and passé. I'm still trying to work on what this confusion is and where it is coming from (stay tuned for an essay or blog post about it some day), but my initial instincts are that Western society has a real love–hate relationship with authoritarian leadership styles and bluff and bluster. This plays out in the writing community as much as anywhere.

So if you're going to read writing life books and get some use from them, it's important to learn the difference between someone telling you what they think and what works for them and telling you exactly what to do. Some writers are more than forceful about this than others in their books, but even so, it's important for you to understand: No one is telling you what to do. They are telling you what worked for them.

Let's take writing first drafts by hand, for example. Heather Sellers, one of my writing life heroes and colleagues, makes a very strong case for this practice in her book *Page by Page*. If I wanted to, I could really get my hackles up over her argument, because, while I used to write exclusively by hand years ago (yes, I began writing before computers were a thing) in the last ten years I have switched over to typing on a keyboard and I just am not so sure about bowing down to the God of handwriting. I go into a sort of reverie when I type, the sort of artist's "flow" that Mikhail Csikszentmihalyi describes in his famous creativity research—I always have—it feels very meditative to me. So I'm just not sure I agree with Sellers. That's ok. I'm taking the idea into consideration—I'm still thinking about it—and I don't think that in her passion for drafting by hand, Sellers is "telling me what to do." She's telling me what *she* does and what works for her. I respect her so I'm just keeping this idea open for now—I haven't made up my mind about it. In fact, the ability to hold two opposing ideas in our minds— known as "negative capability"—will serve you well as an artist.

So, let's be clear: I am not now, not ever, going to tell you the one way to write. There is no one way to write, and if anyone else tells you that there is, they are either deluded or lying through their teeth. I am going to tell you in the pages to come what has worked for me in building a writing life in the hopes that some of it may inspire you or at least save you a little—maybe even a lot—of trouble. But I am not telling you what to do. I am telling you what I did. When you come across something in this book that strikes an off note with you, I ask you to do the same thing—keep an open mind. Because ultimately, in spite of the fact that I disagree with Heather Sellers on handwriting, *Page by Page* still shares shelf space with a handful of my most beloved books on writing. I pull it off and thumb through it whenever I need encouragement. All of these books hold ideas that fill my soul and all of them contain a few ideas that leave me a little hungry, still. That's how ideas work. Take some into your heart and let others pass right through.

Notes

1 "Harry Potter Nerds Win At Life." YouTube Video, 3:31. Posted by Vlogbrothers, July 19, 2009. https://www.youtube.com/watch?v=rMweXVWB918

2 Shanley, John Patrick. *Moonstruck*, directed by Norman Jewison. 1987. Beverly Hills, CA: MGM DVD, 2011.

1

Making the commitment

You don't always choose writing. Sometimes writing chooses you. Sometimes it grabs you by the lapels, gets in your face, and keeps you awake at night, assuring you won't rest until you get your thoughts down, somehow. Sometimes it just feels like a constant malaise, a low-grade depression, like you're forgetting something, leaving something behind, by not writing. Sometimes it feels like a slow build-up of thoughts and words until it feels as if your head, or your heart, might burst. You know you have to do something. You just don't know how or what.

Over the years, I've learned to respect the feeling. Sometimes, I simply had to start an essay even if it was eleven o'clock on a Thursday night and even if the essay ended up going nowhere. Sometimes I just felt frustrated and angsty until I realized that for one reason or another, I hadn't written anything in a few days. A week. A few weeks.

Before I go further, though, let me tell you a story, a cautionary tale, if you will, about what might happen if you ignore the signs that you're the kind of person who will be better off if you make a space for writing in your life. If you don't bat the signs away like gnats, telling yourself you're not a "real" writer after all or you don't have the time.

Did you ever hear the one about the brain surgeon who approaches a novelist at a cocktail party and says, "A novelist, huh? Someday I'm going to take a couple of weeks off and write a novel." Whereupon the novelist replies, "What a coincidence. I always thought that someday I might like to take a couple of weeks off and try some brain surgery."

The fact that I first heard this joke thirty years ago and it's still making the rounds is testament to the way writing is viewed in our society: That producing a novel is easy and anyone can do it given a little time and a cabin in the woods, the way Rob Petrie sets out to do (or famously, "not do") in the classic episode of the eponymous *Dick Van Dyke Show*. In actuality, anyone who doesn't put in the time that a writing apprenticeship requires is only setting themselves up for disappointment.

Take Tom. Tom was a successful lawyer in the mid-sized southern city where I did my graduate work twenty years ago. He was also fighting a brain tumor. Writing a novel had always been on his bucket list. Given the exigencies of Tom's situation, he'd actually sat down and written the thing, a John Grisham-esque legal thriller, and then hired a succession of my graduate student-writer friends to help him whip it into shape. One of his last wishes was to see it published.

By all accounts, Tom was a great guy, he was smart, self-effacing, funny, and kind, and his generosity to the poor graduate students who worked with him was legendary—for example, he scheduled many a "working lunch" with them at some of the best restaurants in town. Everyone who knew him adored him. And to a person, every poor graduate student who worked with him thought his legal thriller was hopeless. You could tell it pained them to admit it, because they were so fond of him, but the thing wasn't salvageable; they wished it was. Keep in mind, this was the mid-nineties, before publishing on demand was even a flicker in anyone's eye. No one thought Tom was going to be able to cross this particular item off his list.

Fortunately, Tom had crossed a lot of other important stuff off the list. He'd had a successful legal career, friends who'd do anything for him, the abiding love of his wife and children and ultimately, that's what really mattered. By all accounts, his funeral was a spectacular celebration of a life truly well-lived. But if publishing a novel was really something he'd wanted to do in life, he waited too late. Far, far too late.

Because writing is a marathon, not a sprint.

Alan Cheuse used to tell his students that most writers needed to write several hundred thousand throwaway words before they'd even begin to produce their best work. *Several hundred thousand words.* The number seemed daunting to my twenty-three-year-old ears, yet, freeing as well: Every crappy writing session I put in after that could be chalked up to meeting that gargantuan word count. Thirty years on, it sounds about right to me. But the idea is this: Once you've decided to be a writer, you have to figure out a way to do it and you have to keep doing it, especially while you learn, which can take a long time. A lifetime, even, because I'm still learning—I'll always be learning.

Don't wait until you have a few years to live. It's not enough time.

I have written since I could hold a crayon. Sometimes I attracted the attentions of a teacher, like Mr McCann, but more often than not I plodded away, pining for a bone here and there. In eleventh grade I wrote a story about a beautiful librarian in love in a seaside town (fortunately, that's all I can remember) and actually won honorable mention in a teen magazine for it. About eight other teen writers won honorable mention too but that kept me going for a while, since most of my teachers were ignoring me.

I was a quiet, unassuming student who wanted nothing more than a few encouraging words form my teachers and rarely got them—in fact, I was underestimated throughout my elementary- and high-school years, which, when you get right down to it, is pretty good training for a writer.

College was better, but I still kept my writing under wraps. You had to apply to Blanche Boyd's Introductory Fiction class at Connecticut College and carving out the solitude to write that story as a first-year student was my first experience with the whole "rising at dawn" to make time to write experiment. Looking back, I still can't believe I got in with the story I wrote—it was still on the level of "beautiful librarians"—but I would develop more quickly after that.

Those classes were the first time I went semi-public with my writing and it wasn't easy—I think that's why I'm sympathetic to the young writers I teach today. For the first few months, I was sick to my stomach before each session. I was so worried that I would write something unworthy of the workshop that I begged Blanche (or Ms Boyd, as I insisted on calling her then, even though she urged us to call her by her first name) to preview every single story I wrote and to stop me from submitting it to workshop if she thought I might humiliate myself in front of the whole class. To this day, I'm deeply grateful that she honored what, in retrospect, seems like a ridiculous request. But I suppose asking Blanche to "stop me before I embarrass myself," was my own way of asking, like my students do, "Do I have what it takes? Am I allowed to be a writer?"

In my senior year, I openly applied to graduate programs in my major, Developmental Psychology (and got into Columbia, my sole opportunity to brag about being accepted into an Ivy), and secretly applied to several Master of Fine Arts (MFA) creative writing programs. Yes, secretly. George Mason University was my first choice because Richard Bausch taught there and I had been studying his work for a while, on Blanche's recommendation. I told myself that this would be the real test. If I got into an MFA program, it would mean I could hack it as a writer; if I didn't, well, then I could just hang it up and no one would have to know.

Look at me, testing myself over and over again. Why do we do this? Why is it so hard to just say, "yes, I'm a writer. Because I write"?

Easy for me to say. I'm in my forties. I ought to feel like I have permission by now. But I still remember when I didn't.

I don't want you to have to wait that long.

You don't need to hear from me or anyone else. You just need to do it. And you need to make the space in your life. Let me give you a couple of suggestions.

Life partners

I was waxing philosophically in the car one day with my oldest son (which is where, many parents will tell you, a lot of philosophical waxing tends to take place) when I mentioned that I thought two of the most important things in life were finding the right life partner and finding fulfilling work.

He sat quietly for a few moments in the backseat, mulling this over. He was about ten at the time. Finally he asked, "What if you don't want a life partner?"

Oops. Okay, then. Family, finding a partner, having children, these were things I wanted from the time I was very young. It never occurred to me that my son wouldn't want the same thing, although given how independent and solitary he has always been, I suppose I shouldn't have been surprised. As usual, in his insistence yet again on *not being me*, he was teaching me that we're not all the same and we don't all want the same things.

That was some years ago and now that he's on the other side of puberty, he's revised his position somewhat. But my point is, not everyone wants or needs a partner, so skip this section if that person would be you. If you're more like me, however, and a life partner was always in the plan, I cannot emphasize enough the importance of finding the right one. I've known people who were and were not successful in this decision and if you want to pursue a writing life, it really matters.

I can't say whether my choice was all that deliberate except that I let some early partners go that simply were not supportive of my work or just didn't understand what I was trying to do. The high-school boyfriend who was such a traditionalist that anything I did was always going to take a second or third or fourth seat to his plans. The college boyfriend who had a long list of stellar qualities but who just wasn't interested in literature or writing—at all—which was ultimately a deal breaker. The brief interlude right after college with he who shall not be named, who loved his vintage Z28 more than just about anything else, but the less said about him the better.

And then there was the guy who came along right after that, my husband, who is so perfect for me the universe might as well have wrapped him up in foil and taped a bow to his head.

There. Now you know how ridiculously, geekily, schoolgirl crazy I am about my husband after nearly thirty years. But you also need to know why he's the perfect partner for any writer or artist, so you can look for similar qualities:

1. He supports what I do

Well, he'd probably draw the line if my life's goal were to become a top-ranked kitten-juggler (he *loves* cats), but otherwise he understands that writing is something that needs to have a place in my life. He doesn't resent it. He doesn't snicker at it. It doesn't threaten him in any way. He's not standing behind me while I work, wondering when I'm going to make it pay or at least do something useful, like empty the dishwasher. He leaves me alone to do what I need to do.

2. He believes in equality in a partnership

I shouldn't have to write this in the twenty-first century, but if you're going to be able to carve out time for writing, especially if you're a woman, you must have a partner who believes the work of family life should be shared. You would be surprised how many women I've known over the years whose writing time evaporated once they got married, and especially once they had children, because their partner assumed they'd also picked up a shirt-presser, suitcase packer, dishwasher, chef, and full-time nanny in the bargain. My husband and I are both writers and full-time university professors. He does his own laundry, irons his own shirts, cooks most of our meals (his choice—which says a lot about my cooking—while I do cleanup), would be horrified if I went near one of his suitcases, and does as much or more for our children as I do.

On the flip side, there are also women out there who would expect the man of the household to be out bringing home the big bucks in a high-powered career that would allow them to work as a stay-at-home parent. High-powered careers don't usually leave much time for writing.

You get the picture. Choose a partner who supports your vision (and vice versa) and divide the labor in any way that makes sense to you both, but divide it more or less evenly or your writing will take a hit.

3. He is also a writer, immensely talented and dedicated

I realize not everyone can marry a writer but I highly recommend it. Fellow writers understand what you're trying to do, what you need to do, and why you need to do it. There's no learning curve when you take up with another writer. They get it.

In my case, another benefit to being married to this particular writer is that he is the hardest-working writer I know. When he's not doing all the wonderful things I mentioned above, or being a great writing teacher, he's writing. Constantly. During the school year, he usually gets up at 4 a.m. to make sure he puts in his time at his desk. 4 a.m.! This makes it almost impossible for me to slack off or complain. After all, he's finding the time to do it. Why can't I? I just do my best to keep up.

4. He doesn't have a competitive or jealous bone in his body

My husband and I met in a writing workshop and have since been in many others together. People always marveled at how supportive we were of each other, that we never sniped at each other or seemed jealous of one another. This mystified us. When you love someone, all you want is for them to be happy and fulfilled. Right? That's what makes you happy. Nothing gives me more joy than celebrating with him over a book contract or a great review. I'm his biggest fan. I always will be. And he's mine. Whether or not we shared the same profession, I hope that would always be true.

So I realize that there may not be enough writers for everyone, and there's certainly only one John Vanderslice, but I hope you get the message that it's important to share your life with someone who is willing to do the extra work that's required so that you're fulfilled, just as you are willing to do for them. You want someone who makes your dreams their own.

If your relationship doesn't exactly fit these parameters, I'm not suggesting you call it quits with your partner. But sharing this section of the book with them, sitting down together and making a plan for how you're going to support each other in leading fulfilling lives might be a good idea. And if you're still looking for a partner, perhaps now you have a good sense of what to look for.

Oh, and some of you who follow the independent music scene might have already realized I wasn't being totally straight with you when I said there was only one John Vanderslice. There actually is another one and he's a famous indie rocker. No kidding. Google him.

I have no idea how that one rates as a partner. Although it's hard to imagine he's better than mine.

Financial planning

If you haven't figured it out by now, this would be a good time to tell you that living a writing life isn't necessarily conducive to living in an outrageously expensive city, carrying a hefty mortgage or having a luxury car payment, unless you're a hedge fund manager or anesthesiologist who likes to write on the side. It's entirely possible to manage your vocations and your avocations this way: Poet William Carlos Williams was a doctor, Jeff Kinney, who writes the *Diary of a Wimpy Kid* series, is a video-game designer and clearly feels no guilt about hogging not one but two cool careers. But they're the exceptions to the rule.

Still, if you want to write, think hard about whether you need to live in Manhattan, where you might have to have two or three jobs to support yourself while you share an apartment with three other people, or whether you can write and do whatever else you need to do to support your word habit in a location where it might be a little easier to get by. One of my former students, Gus Carlson, the graphic novelist behind *Backwoods Folk* and other comics, lives in a cabin in the middle of the Ozarks, which, as long as it has wifi, seems to suit him fine as he builds his career.

Another student didn't strategize so well. Turns out the assistantship he got to pursue graduate study in writing didn't stretch to cover the payments on the new car he'd bought. Rather than ditch the car for something more affordable, he ditched the graduate program and switched to something more immediately lucrative, though not necessarily fulfilling. I didn't own a new car until I was thirty-three and midway through the tenure track: Until then my wheels consisted of a reliable, supremely un-cool Chevy Cavalier (literally and figuratively; the car had no air conditioning the entire time we lived in subtropical Louisiana) and then a Saturn Station Wagon—which screamed: "WE ARE SO UNCOOL WE CAN'T EVEN HAGGLE." Both painted a conservative navy blue, driving these cars was the equivalent of cruising in a Catholic school uniform. The point is, they got me and my husband through two advanced degrees and eight years of full-on attention to our development as writers. Five years from now, what will my former student have? A used car and a job he doesn't like.

I'm not saying you have to live on ramen noodles for the rest of your life or take a vow of poverty. I'm just suggesting a little strategy, a little delayed gratification, as you figure out how to build writing into your life and support yourself at the same time.

Family planning

For some people, the idea of eventually having children is non-negotiable. I would be one of those people. Legend has it that at seven, I informed my mother that if I wasn't married by a certain age, I would adopt anyway because I was having children no matter what. Keep in mind that I made this proclamation in the late 1970s, when having a husband *and* children was still the official script. Keep in mind the idea behind *why* I might even need to adopt was still a few years off, along with a more solid understanding of the science of conception.

Knowing my mother as I do, I'm sure she was proud of my budding feminism and secretly thought that claiming to have "lost" the instructions to the Barbie Dream House I received for my fifth birthday—which meant it never made it out of the box—had finally paid off. But I was quite serious. There were two things I have always known I wanted in life. To have a family and to write.

It helps to know what you want so that you can be mindful and plan for it, so that biology does not become your destiny. This means that whether you are a man or a woman, if children aren't high on your list for fulfillment, do whatever makes sense to you to avoid having them. Conversely, if having children is important to you, you might not want to put it off for too long. Whatever makes sense for you. Having children was a conscious decision for my husband and me, something we both wanted. Because infertility runs in my family, it wasn't something we thought we could casually defer. Children also require attention, care, and feeding and since we were both in the early stages of our writing development, we knew we'd have to develop other careers to support them, both of us. We waited about three years after we were married, when we had been writing for a while and were well into the graduate programs that would help us eventually find university teaching jobs, before we had our first child. I was twenty-nine and my husband was thirty-five. We could have started earlier and we could have started later. Plenty of people do. But we also wanted more than one, so we knew we couldn't wait too long.

Beginning our family at this point introduced certain obligations and definitely made some aspects of both of our writing lives more difficult, but we wouldn't have done anything differently. In our son's first year, my husband and I both finished creative/critical dissertations, started to publish, and probably applied to close to 300 academic jobs between us. It was completely exhausting but I wouldn't trade that miraculous first year with our son for anything in the world.

As luck would have it, he was a preternaturaly good baby who slept—I am not kidding—twelve hours a night from two months on, which did allow us to get some work done. Lest this fact make you want to stare poison darts at my husband and me, however, be reassured that our second child utterly made up for his brother's somnolence by an unwillingness to miss a single moment, even if it meant poking his own eyes with his tiny fingers and spitting his pacifier across the room in desperate attempts to keep himself awake.

This second child was born early in my writing career, when I was pre-tenure, because we were worried (again, we are not an especially fecund couple and some years had passed) that if we didn't stay in the game we'd only have the one and we really wanted more than that (my husband is one of eight and I was a clichéd "lonely only"). As it was, the second one's conception required a lot more pharmacological intervention than the first, so it was a good thing we didn't wait for the post-tenure baby I'd always fantasized about but who never would come to be.

What I'm getting at is that neither of these periods in our lives were the "ideal" times to have a child. With the first, we were staring down total job insecurity, with no idea where we'd be living or working by his first birthday; with the second, the consequences of getting dinged for tenure with not one but now two little people to feed never left my thoughts for a moment. But most parents will tell you, there really isn't ever a "perfect" time and if you want a family, sometimes you just have to take the plunge. Biological clocks, for women especially, can't be stopped and there are upper limits, in many places, to the age at which you can adopt.

Over the years I've met a few writers, all men, who suggested they had to sacrifice having a family for their art. One of them, a very famous writer, in fact, who you have probably heard of, also added to this proclamation that he could not write and teach at the same time. And he taught one class per year, one night a week, with no more than fifteen students in it. Let's be honest here. Obviously these people did not want a family very much, and there's nothing wrong with that. But people who do will find a way to have both. The list of people who have accomplished this feat is exhaustive and includes winners of every literary prize you can imagine, including the Nobel.

While we're at it, let's also address the myth that every child a woman has means one less book she could have written. Sorry, but I'm just not buying it. Replace the word "woman" with the word "man" and the whole idea sounds preposterous, laughable even. And it's wrong. There are many female writers, first of all, who are fairly prolific and who have passels of children: Susan Shreve, Julianna Baggott, Donna Jo Napoli, Beth Ann Fennelly, Shirley Jackson. Really, I'm just getting started.

I'll get more into the rhythms of family life and writing in the next chapter but let me tell you, without qualification, having children is no more an excuse for writing fewer books than not having children a reason for writing more of them. In fact, many writing mothers and fathers will tell you that having children helps them to be more judicious about how they spend their time, writing or otherwise.

So families, yes. If you want one, don't deny yourself. Just try to plan. And be ready to modify and adjust, because we all know what the universe thinks of plans.

Mind-altering substances

Tread with the utmost care here. Drugs and alcohol have ruined the lives and shortened the careers of far more writers than they have ever helped. In fact, after several decades in the literary world, I can say with certainty that I know of no writer who ever wrote a truly great work under the influence or who wrote anything of much worth at all under the influence. Most writers will agree with me on this, and those who do not most likely struggle with addiction themselves, if they are honest about it.

While I tried various libations in my youth—from the neophyte White Russians of my late teens to Screwdrivers (with Stolichnaya vodka, of course, it was the 80s, after all) to the Bass Ales and hard ciders I drank abroad, anyone who knows me will tell you white wine is my signature drink. And while I enjoy a nice glass of sauvignon blanc or two or occasionally, three, as much as anyone else I know (perhaps more), I also know that once I take that first drink, it's unlikely that I'm going to get any useful writing done. I've tried; it never comes to any good. My thinking just isn't clear enough after that and writing requires clarity of thought more than anything else. Alcohol also makes me weary, eventually, also not a state conducive to making art.

In terms of other mind-altering substances, I lived in Washington, D.C., in the early 90s where I was treated to the effects of the drug crisis through the daily pages of the *Washington Post Metro* section and the stark realization that there was an entire underclass paying for any lily-white bourgeois experimentation pretty much put an end to that. In the years afterwards I've gotten to know people who've struggled mightily with addiction and learned just how lucky I have been—with the genes for dependence scattered throughout my family tree as much as anyone else's— to have dodged that particular bullet. So listen hard when I tell you that there is perhaps no myth more common or more damaging than that the use and/or abuse of drugs and alcohol is somehow critical to artistic enlightenment, if only because it seems that a fair number of beginning writers still fall for it.

Beginning writers who never progress further and often end up in rehab and fighting that demon for the rest of their lives. Don't risk it, yourself, or your art.

Don't start down that lonesome road.

It's a marathon, not a sprint, redux

As we've established, writing is a long apprenticeship. Remember Alan Cheuse and his several hundred thousand words? This can come as hard news for some, especially a writer's family members, who often hold the misguided notion that the royalty checks will start rolling in fairly quickly if the writer has, "what it takes." Fortunately, however, unlike say, modeling, pro-football, or Olympic gymnastics, there's no time limit. You won't be washed up and robbing convenience stores at thirty-five. You'll probably just be hitting your stride.

So are you patient? Good. Patience is probably the number one job requirement for a writer—along with the ability to (occasionally) forego sleep and to soldier on through failure and rejection for a reward that may or may not come for a couple of decades.

Wait a minute ... that job description sounds an awful lot like ... parenthood. Or anything that requires dedication without an immediate payoff, or the promise of any payoff, really, in the end. You simply have to have to love the process of doing it more than anything else, more than the payoff. The same is true for any art.

My second child, the insomniac, developed an abiding passion for cello in his teens, such that he decided at fourteen he wanted to make this his career. Because we knew nothing about this particular art, we sought advice from the cellist at our university, Dr Stephen Feldman, who has since become his mentor and teacher. One of the things Dr Feldman stressed to our son at their first meeting was that he needed to be pursuing music for the love of doing it, for the love of expressing himself through this instrument—not for the money, or for the accolades, or the visions of glory because none of those things, even if he was one of the lucky few who were fortunate to attain them, would ultimately sustain him for the long haul, the hours and hours of practicing, the exhaustion, and sometimes the rejection and defeat. But the love of doing it—that would carry him all of his days.

As I sat and listened, it was with the great relief that I had trusted my young cellist to exactly the right person.

2

Doing the work (and, sometimes, not doing the work)

Finding the time

Once you've made the big changes—right partner (if you want one), check; relatively low overhead, check; children, present or not present and accounted for, check—assuming that you don't write full time, how do you make the small changes in your life so that you can actually do the writing? The solutions are actually kind of straightforward—but unfortunately, not necessarily easy. Stay up late, get up early, and cut stuff out.

Staying up late

This is a common option for a lot of people and before I had children, it was my go-to solution. My husband is an early bird and for the first several years of our marriage, we shared an office and a computer. Since I was a night owl, it made sense that I used the office in the evening, after he went to bed, while he used it in the early mornings. Our writing chair rarely grew cold. After children, however, especially after our second child, this option became difficult for me. As the night owl, I am also the night-time parent, which means I do all the bedtime wrangling and my husband handles the early risers. This was straightforward with our first child, who ran full throttle from around 6 a.m. and then fell into a deep sleep by early evening. His sleeping habits left a solid couple of hours each evening when I could get some good work done.

By contrast, our second child's response to everything about the life we had created with his brother seemed to be, "Not so fast." This included sleeping schedules. Not only was he a night owl, just like me, but he recognized from an early age that the best way to have me all to himself was to stay up later than anyone else in the house. Suffice it to say that we have had a lot of bonding time over the years. In my ongoing efforts to lull him to sleep I read to him long after he could read to himself, choosing books for their style as much as their content, so that in reading aloud great stylists like E. B. White, Kate DiCamillo, and Brian Selznick, I was also training my ear.

Unfortunately, I also discovered that after a cozy read aloud of *The Miraculous Journey of Edward Tulane*, a long writing session was not likely to happen. Actually, what was most likely to happen was that I'd wake up in my son's room around 2 a.m. wondering where I was. Writing time had to be found another way.

Getting up early

Eventually, I had to start getting up early. Really early. At first the thought was utterly repulsive. Have I mentioned that I am not a morning person? For most of my life, being conscious before the sun has come up has brought on waves of existential nausea. It just feels wrong. I avoided it until I could avoid it no longer. It was the only way I could get any writing done.

It took time to get my body on board with this new schedule. I had to bribe myself with a big ol' honking mug of French-pressed coffee. I still do. For me, there is no writing, no thinking, without coffee. I also had to start looking at what at first felt like a painful time in a different way. I was giving something to myself. Something I really needed. Time to write and time to be quiet in my own head became a reward in itself, something worth dragging myself out of bed for. Although it's still easier to do during the times of the year when the sun is already up.

Here's the thing about getting up early, though, or about anything that seriously cuts into your body's ability to rejuvenate. You have to be judicious about it. Unless you're like my husband, who expires before 9 each night, if you get up very early, you will be burning the proverbial candle at both ends. If I have a long day or especially an evening event—and as a professor who wears many hats at my university, I often do—I've learned I need to give myself that extra hour or two of sleep in the morning so I can power through those events with a smile on my face. This means that sometimes I pursue my early morning routine only once, maybe twice, a week. Also—my kids are older now and no longer need me at night so I am back to my old ways in that regard. I'm older too—not as good at depriving myself as I was ten years ago—and that affects the work schedule.

The other reason I only recommend cutting back on sleep a few times a week, at most, is that more and more research shows that a decent night's sleep is important to good health and long life. It's a factor in maintaining a healthy weight, healthy blood pressure, and so on. So if you cut back on sleep too much, too often, you may take some years off your life on the other end and that would sort of defeat the purpose if you want a long lifetime of writing. Look into other places to find time—maybe an hour or two on Saturday and Sunday— to feed your soul and round out the word count.

While we're talking about health, I might as well throw in my
theory on exercise and writing time. I think exercise is important. I try
to get in about forty-five minutes three to four times a week depending
on what my workload is like. I have done this since college, in part
because of my glacially slow metabolism. If I don't, I am guaranteed to
start packing on pounds; it's how I'm built. I also do this in part
because I'm married to a dedicated runner and being married to a
dedicated runner has a similar effect to being married to a dedicated
writer. It's hard to feel good about lounging on the sofa when your
partner is jogging out the door.

Still, I struggle with this time when I think about writers I know
who don't exercise regularly and who don't outwardly seem to need to.
To be honest, I'm jealous. When you add getting into and out of
workout clothes, traveling back and forth to the gym, you're talking
about at least an hour and a half a day, three times a week. Four and a
half hours that could be spent writing. No small thing. It doesn't seem
fair. But heart disease and type two diabetes and a whole host of other
ailments of the unfit run in my family. I rationalize that I'm putting
years of writing back at the other end of my life by exercising now.
Years, I hope, of feeling strong and being active. That's where I'm
putting my money, anyway.

On *not* writing

In case I'm beginning to sound a bit writing-crazed at this point, let me
stop and tell you that if you're trying to fit writing into your life, unless
you are independently wealthy and have your own domestic staff, there
will be times when you won't be able to do it. Times when you'll need to
be kind to yourself and let it go—for a little while. Times when you've
suffered a great loss and need to heal. Times when you've welcomed a
child into your home—whether through birth or adoption (again, we're

not just talking about mothers here)—or when you're dealing with a serious crisis with your family or at work. These are just examples—only you know when to give yourself a break and when you *need* to keep writing in order to process what has happened or even keep your mind off it. I didn't get as much writing done when my kids were babies and toddlers; before they started preschool. This was in part because my husband and I were both exhausted and just trying to get through the day. But it was also because children are only young once and we didn't want to miss too much. It's a simple fact. You don't get those years back.

This is not to say I didn't write at all—that's not possible. I can't not write. I also work at a university where the maxim "publish don't perish" rules, and I wasn't tenured until my youngest child was four. But if productivity were a line graph, you would definitely see an uptick when the youngest started preschool and another when he started kindergarten.

Writing doesn't necessarily need to come before family. Writing comes out of your own time, which does exist; writing is what you do for you. It is not an excuse for neglecting your loved ones, though. I'm reminded of a writing teacher of mine who used to tell the story of getting a call at his writing desk one day that there had been a chemical spill near his children's school and that concerned parents could come and pick up their children if they wished. To demonstrate the sanctity of his writing time, he claimed that his next question was, "Which way is the wind blowing?"

I'm not sure I believe this story; it always sounded apocryphal to me, another form of writerly chest-beating. As a parent, I find it even harder to imagine. Not long after the Columbine shooting, my son's preschool called me at work to tell me that the local high school next door was being evacuated due to a bomb threat and it was recommended we come for our own children. I don't remember much between hanging up the phone and driving away from that school with a dazed but safe toddler in the back seat but to this day, one of my colleagues claims she's never seen anyone move so fast.

Writer's block is also infamous, of course, though it hasn't tormented me too much. This is not to say words have not often been a struggle—one mark of a writer is that's usually the case—but I've rarely been unable to write at all. But it happens, often when something else traumatic is going on. The September 11 attacks are the best example for me. My uncle, who has been an important person in my life, worked in the Towers, although by some miracle, he was late to work that day. The closest he got was a bus in the Bowery as the second plane was hitting. The time between when I found out about the attack and when I learned he was safe was mercifully brief, about ten minutes, but my entire extended family—mother, grandmother, aunts, uncles, cousins—lives in New York, Queens, and Long Island, specifically. It feels almost as much like home to me as where I actually grew up. For the first few weeks after the attacks, it was difficult to even get phone calls through. I was frantic with worry. If you were alive and aware during that time, you remember. We all were.

For a while after that, at least six months, the words just would not come. There didn't seem to be any point. Bin Laden and the bespectacled al-Zawahiri were in our faces throughout the twenty-four-hour news cycle, promising newer, broader attacks. Then the Anthrax crisis, an eight-month-old infant stricken at NBC studios. Every day brought a new scare, Bush, Cheney, Rumsfeld appearing ashen at the podium of yet another of what turned out to be an endless march of press conferences. I remember praying that my children, then five and one, would actually have a future. I remember setting small goals. If we can just make it through Christmas without another attack. If we can just make it to the family reunion in July.

It seems strange now, as a person who has always processed the world through writing, to have been without words during this national trauma. Especially since a lot of writers *were* writing, beautifully, about it. That's not the only national trauma that has made my creative spirit waver either—the world can be a turbulent place. But eventually I started to feel that old restlessness again, eventually I started to feel that invisible hand at my back, gently urging me to my desk. And I learned something. If I followed my own instincts and trusted myself, the words would return. Unfortunately, there are times in your life when a trauma or crisis arrives that requires every ounce of emotional energy you possess. For some people, making art is the only way to deal with something like this; for others, there is simply nothing left to direct toward the considerable energy it takes to create. If you're in the latter group, this might be a good time to try some revision or editing, something that helps you stay in the game until you can muster the strength to get back to work. Or give yourself a break. One way or another, you just have to hold that scratchy burlap sack of pain in your arms and believe me when I tell you, over time it's going to get lighter and lighter, until eventually you'll be able to let it go. Trust that one day your hands will finally be free to write again.

What writing does come before

I talk to students a lot about the challenges of finding time to write. I even assign essays on the subject. Some beginning writers, however, seem to feel that these essays are beneath them and will shrug them off as the stuff of amateurs. Real writers never need help finding time to write. Yet often, it is these very same writers who will later complain to me that a class, university, or real-life requirement is making it hard for them to get any writing done.

The problem is these beginning writers labor under the myth that somehow, someday, it will actually get easier for them, that someone will want them to write, will pull out their chair and beckon them to sit down—and if they can just hang in there, nurturing their dazzling talent until that time, they will be fine. They could not be more wrong. It only gets harder—even for best-selling authors, for people who write full-time. Even these people must protect their time from those who want them to do other things—mentoring, book promotion, you name it. That's why we need to remember all the things writing *must* come before.

In *Bird by Bird: Some Instructions on Writing and Life*, Anne Lamott wrote that if you could just give up the 10 o'clock news, you could reclaim enough time for your writing. But *Bird by Bird* was written in 1993, before digital media had saturated our lives. We live in a different world now. Now, writing must not only come before the 10 o'clock news, it must come before social media and subscription TV, it must come before binge-watching anything. It must come before YouTube and the latest reality show. It must come before the latest video game, it must come before your *favorite* video game. It must come before happy hour, before most parties, and most lunches with friends. It must come before most hobbies, it comes before retail therapy, and it comes before surfing the Internet, unless you're doing research.

I'm not kidding. In order to have time for writing in your life, as well as for your family and a sustaining job, you must limit distractions. I have a quota on lunches with friends—I try to keep them to one per week. I don't go out much on weekends unless it's to literary events; I stay home to spend time with my family, write, catch up on work, or read (note: Neither my husband nor I worked as much on weekends when our kids were young; we only do so now that they are interested in other pursuits). I watch one to three "appointment" TV shows per week, a home movie every Friday night with the family, and have a date night at home with my husband every Saturday (what can I say— our family is pretty ritual-bound). I go to church many Sundays to feed my soul, but my denomination is such that I don't spend the whole day there (and sometimes, when I do volunteer work for church in the same week, I count that as my church and skip the Sunday devotional). Otherwise, when I am not working my day job (teaching writing) on vacation (a few weeks a year), I spend time with my family, write, and read, in that order. And while that might *sound* like a life devoid of leisure; I can think of few more fulfilling ways to spend my time: On what I truly love. That *is* my leisure.

Hobby-free zones, messy houses, and appointments: More tricks of the trade

Let me say this again because you need to hear it. No one wants you to write. Some people, like your boss or your parents, are all smiles when you have written, but no one wants you to write. They want you to go to lunch with them, they want you to come do some writing lessons with their fourth graders, they want you to read and then write comments on their talented nephew's nine-hundred-page fantasy masterpiece, but they do not want you to actually write. It's not really their fault, they just don't understand how hard it is to defend your writing time against the forces that would nibble it into oblivion. But I *do* want you to write, and I have some suggestions.

First, give up the idea of having many outside hobbies. This is not to say that writing is a hobby but it is your passion and it's difficult to maintain a passion and a lot of other hobbies. As someone whose idea of an indulgent Saturday afternoon is flipping aimlessly through crafts books and magazines describing how to make a Louis Vuitton knock off with duct tape plastic wrap, and last Sunday's comics (I'm not making that up; that is, for real, an actual craft), this is a struggle for me. I spend half my time saying, "Wow, that is cute, I could make that," and the other half reminding myself, "Yes, but do you really want to give up two hours of writing time to do it?"

The answer is usually no. I may own several cabinets full of quirky craft supplies and assemblage bits that "might come in handy for a project someday," (in fact, I own a lovely bone folder I have never used. Go ahead. Google "bone folder,") but most of them are either in pristine condition or have only been used once. Once as in, "Ok, that was fun. Now, back to the writing."

Also, unless you have an obsessive neat freak as a partner who is willing to pick up the slack, you might want to give up the idea of a spotlessly clean house, the kind you see in magazines or in the homes of people who: 1. have OCD; 2. have nothing better to do; or 3. can afford considerable help. Obtaining such a house requires a huge time investment that is simply not compatible to getting writing done. Instead, you are going to have to cultivate the ability to willfully ignore the pile of books next to the bed begging to be returned to their shelves and resist the urge to reorganize the kitchen cabinets regularly, even though we were all trained as children (at least the female among us) to believe that organizing canned goods is a productive use of an afternoon.

I'm not saying you've got to live in a pigsty, just that you've got to settle on the degree of mess you and the health department or the other people you live with are comfortable with and work toward maintaining that. If you can afford it, hiring a semi-regular house-cleaner is a valuable investment; I cannot recommend it enough. Once my husband and I could swing it, which wasn't until well into our thirties, we hired someone to do basic cleaning on our house for three hours twice a month. It's not as expensive as you might think and the difference it makes in the quality of our lives is palpable. First, it forces *us* to clean twice a month for the housecleaner, which means both of us taking an hour to put things where they belong and toss the clutter.

Second, because our housecleaner is extremely efficient, it takes her three hours to address of a level of accumulated household dirt and dust that it used to take my husband and me one whole Saturday to get ahead of, which results in more time together or writing.

We've had this service for almost twenty years now and it's survived several rounds of belt-tightening as the cost of living rises and our professor salaries don't. We may cut the locally grown co-op delivery, or the cable service or the cell phone, but my husband knows the cleaning service is not negotiable. As long as we draw breath and an income, we are coming home to clean sheets twice a month.

A paragraph on the merits of outsourcing your housecleaning might seem utterly erroneous to writing and might also shout privilege (does it help that our cars are nine and sixteen years old?) but that only highlights the importance of the concept. Not only does this kind of service give you back several hours of writing time in a direct trade, it also allows you to walk past the stack of bills on the counter or overlook the errant sock on the floor on the way to your desk, knowing that will be taken care of all at once, before the housecleaner comes. There's a lot to be said for letting tasks like these aggregate before you deal with them. Nothing eats away at your daily writing time more than stopping for "just a minute," to fold the laundry. Or going through the junk mail that's been piling up. Or dusting that tchotchke your great-aunt gave you. And. And.

You get the picture.

The bottom line is, it's very easy for writing time to get eaten up, time you've fought so hard for, time you risen early for, stayed up late for—devoured by other tasks simply because, in the moment they seemed easier to do than writing which, while fulfilling, we all know takes a lot of effort and mental energy. Don't let this happen! Here is a final list of tasks that you *must not do* until after you have written:

You must not, I repeat, must not, check your email. Email controls you. You do not control it. While you are writing, you need to be in control. Don't open it. Just don't.

If you are active on social media, participating on sites like Facebook, Twitter, or the app of the moment, you must also avoid these during your work. They are an evil time-suck that will hoover up every second you have set aside for your writing (does this sound like the voice of experience or what?). Several apps exist to help you block social media while you're working. The aptly named SelfControl is my favorite, because it allows you to block the specific sites that give you the most trouble (Facebook for me)—but I'll list several more in the Appendix.

Finally, when you sit down to work, act like you're about to take off in a plane and "turn off all electronic devices." This means your cell phone, your home phone, Skype, and just about any electronic device that might interrupt you except what you use to write with, if it happens to be electronic. If you're like me and tend to get easily lost in cyberspace, you might also want to keep a running list of things you need to look up on the Internet *after* your writing session. For example, I was recently trying to remember the trick Hemingway was famous for that helped him get back into his writing each day. I know I could easily look it up but that meant I'd also risk spinning down a cyberspace black hole. So I just typed, "insert Hemingway example here" and made a note to look it up later.

All of this is a detailed way of reiterating that you simply must erect a force field around the space for writing in your life, a distraction-free zone. If you're something of an introvert, you know you need this time by yourself, just you and the words, so your personality and your writing space dovetail nicely. If you're an extrovert, you still need to find a way to focus. Regardless, you have permission. You don't need to ask anyone. You are worthy of the sacrifice.

The secret code

I had a boyfriend once, let's call him Alex, who was a teetotaler. This was not a problem in itself, but whenever we were at a party and someone innocently offered him a beer, instead of just saying no, Alex would sneer, "I don't drink." If they were really unlucky, he might launch into a treatise on the dangers of alcohol. Needless to say he wasn't very popular at parties; no one understood why he felt the need to go into such detail when a simple, "No thanks, what else do you have?" would do.

Even though your intentions are far more pure, you just want to write, not preach; it works the same way when you tell people you can't do something because you're busy writing. This is just not something people want to hear. In fact, chances are, they'll turn right around and repeat your excuse to someone else with air quotes, as in, "Ed can't come to the PTO meeting, he's 'writing'." Quite simply, they don't believe you. Usually, it's because they don't write themselves, because somewhere along the way they gulped the Kool-Aid, along with everyone else, that you have to be anointed to write and they don't remember any ceremony. And because they don't recall being anointed, they don't want to believe you've been either. Long story short, because *they* don't do it, they don't believe you are or should be doing it either. Remember, no one really wants you to write. We all know that writing is something that happens magically, out of thin air.

Writing, then, is like teetotaling. Most people (unless they're writers themselves, which is why it's good to befriend and even marry these people) don't necessarily care whether you do it as long as you don't actually talk about it. So this is what you're going to tell people when they ask you to do something that conflicts with your sacred writing time. Repeat after me.

"I'm sorry. I can't. I have an appointment."

So when that breakfast meeting your boss is hoping everyone will be free for is threatening what little time you have to write, what do you say?

"I'm sorry. I can't. I have an appointment."

She'll find another time for the meeting. And when your sister has asked you to tutor her ten-year-old in English (because you're so good at it) on Wednesdays at 6 even though you write for two hours after work every night, what do you say?

"I'm sorry. I can't. I have an appointment."

She'll find another time that works for both of you—or another tutor.

Good. So keep practicing that. Because you do have an appointment. With your work.

Unfortunately, the other reason we must use this code when we talk about writing is because most people refuse to believe that writing is work. Even National Public Radio hosts, who ought to know better, made this mistake. I once heard Terry Gross interview John Updike, the person singly responsible for some of the best literature of the twentieth century, and observe, referring to a career that had spanned several decades at that point, something along the lines of, "So. You've never had a real job."

To which Updike, ever the patrician New Englander, paused and then softly averred, something like: "No, I don't suppose I have."

Writing may not be the same as digging ditches or cleaning toilets but neither is accounting—or radio interviewing—but they're all work. I challenge anyone who doesn't think writing is real work to actually sit in front of a blank page or screen on a regular basis and produce something someone else will want to read. Then come back and tell me it's not work. Writing may not be manual labor, and it may be work some of us love, which I wish for everyone, but it is definitely work.

OK, I showed up at the desk: Now what?

I have some suggestions to make your time more productive and therefore less agonizing, but before I get into them, I should point out that there have been volumes written about this subject as well as hundreds of websites and apps developed, the most useful of which are listed in the Appendix. Before we move on, however, some of you might have paused when I used the word, "agonizing." Wait a minute. Agonizing? If writing is something you *want* to make time for, why would it be agonizing?

That's a good question, but if you're asking it, it's one you need to settle before we continue because yes, writing can be agonizing, and as a result, your mind will try to trick you into not doing it. This is why you need to be ready to confront your own manipulative little monkey brain and press on.

First, most kinds of creation can at times be painful or difficult because nothing brings you closer to your innermost desires and your greatest fears, especially of failure, than a blank page or a lump of clay. Second, making space for writing does place a certain amount of pressure on the act itself. As a result, showing up when the words don't come can feel excruciating, can make you feel like you're wasting your time. Nothing could be further from the truth, of course, but it's a good idea to keep some techniques in your arsenal that can help you feel productive while you're writing, for inspiration. Notice I didn't write, while you're waiting for inspiration, or "waiting for the muse." I dislike the idea of the muse, it's always seemed rather, "precious," to me. Something that gets in the way. I don't need to personify my work; I just need to do it.

There's always the good old prompt to get you going, or, because elementary school teachers wore out the phrase "writing prompt," decades ago and then stomped on it a few times to make sure it was really dead, what most writers like to refer to as the "self-assignment." A word, a phrase, a question, an image, or an idea that can get you started. The Internet is rotten with these if you search for them (the Appendix provides a list). Be discriminating.

Another key to consistent writing practice is to try to begin each session with some sense of what you want to do or how you want to start. If you're in the middle of a poem, story, essay, or play, you're already over the hump. But if you're starting fresh, it's good to have a list of images that have long inspired you or of scenes you know need to written in your novel. For example, at the beginning stage of this book, I sketched out a basic plan of what I wanted each chapter to be about and the stories and examples I wanted to describe in each, so that I would start each writing session with a purpose.

It's also an old saw that if you can help it, you want to avoid finishing a work session at the very end of a scene or a line, that it helps if you can leave some work left to be done so that you can just pick up where you left off next time. Here's where the Hemingway factoid comes in: Legend has it that he forced himself to stop working mid-sentence so he could easily pick up there when he next sat down to write.

Finally, one of the long-term benefits of making time to write is that your brain will be in writing mode even when you're not writing. Ideas, lines, and whole scenes will come to you unbidden and if you know what's good for you, you'll have to get them down before you lose them, even if it's not your official writing time. For example, in the twenty-four hours since I last worked on this chapter, I thought of three ideas I wanted to add. My subconscious mind is always working on my writing, even when my conscious mind is directing me in taking a shower or driving to a meeting.

To maximize these times, you'll need some sort of receptacle, something to receive that flood of great ideas—a journal, notebook, a legal pad. I'm not talking about a diary in which you chronicle your every thought but an easily accessible place to catch your ideas. Too much has been made in the writing world about diary-keeping. True, there are some writers who love to transcribe every detail of their lives and it can make for great reading after they die (except for the journals of John Cheever, which, in my opinion, are so dark and depressing they would make anyone want to slit their wrists. And I am a big Cheever fan.) But a lot of us don't feel that inclination and we don't need to feel guilty about it. We just need a place to keep our ideas. Because an idea that is not committed to writing is an idea that may vanish forever. Forget, "if it's important, I'll remember it." As a writer, you have a lot of important ideas swirling in your brain—if you don't get them down, you *will* lose some. On January 24, 1998, as I was falling asleep, an idea for what I thought at the time was the best story idea I'd ever had popped into my head. It was like a story idea combined with the secret of life—it was that good. I was tired and didn't think I needed to write it down. It was such a great idea, I was sure I'd remember it.

January 25, 1998, I woke up, all fired up to get started writing it. But what was it?

Damned if I know.

And I was young then. I had not yet crossed the memory-thieving bridge.

It is for this reason that I believe in the writing receptacle—yes, you can use your smartphone too, but the added benefit of hard copy you can hold in your hands is that it makes the archivists happy. I worry about the archivists. How are they going to track down everything being transmitted into the ether today? How are they going to curate the writer's "papers" of the future? I'm sure there are digital archivists toiling away at this problem right this very minute, or at least I hope there are. But until a solution is found, I think we need to leave some hard-copy evidence of our literary existence.

I realize that at this point you are probably thinking, "well, doesn't she think she's all that, assuming that anything she writes is worth archiving?" Not exactly. I've just worked in several historical archives and let me tell you: It's all worth saving. Flyers, dance programs, student papers, grocery lists: The multiple drafts of a poem written by one particular woman at one particular place and time in the early twenty-first century, these can all illuminate the work of historians laboring to piece together our lives 100 years from now. So you. This means you. Your writing is important. As you fill your journals and notebooks, whatever receptacles you choose, find a safe place to keep them. Provide a loved one with instructions on what to do with them when you are no longer around: Keep them for the family to cherish, give them to the local or state historical society, or a local university library. Or, if you are really, truly determined that you don't want anyone to see them, enlist a good friend to burn them for you or clear your hard drives when you die.

This is one of the few times that being a female writer is actually beneficial. We can carry purses without attracting attention and purses are great for holding the various journals that are catcher's mitts for inspiration. Chances are if you've ever expressed the fact that you like to write in front of a friend or family member, you already have a tidy little collection of these that you've received as gifts over the years. Or, if you're like many of us, notebooks to you are like shoes to Imelda Marcos; there's always another, better one beckoning. I keep a box of them in my study and look forward to coming to the end of one notebook just for the opportunity it provides to select the next.

If, whether a man or a woman, the idea of a purse or bag does not appeal, there are also alternatives to journals. You can keep a tiny, palm-sized notebook in your chest or pants pocket—writer Kim Stafford has nice, simple instructions for making these in his book *The*

Muses Among Us and there are others online—or you can try my favorite option, the sticky note.

Before sticky notes came into widespread use, Anne Lamott used to sing the praises of the notecard, a three-by-five card that one could keep handy to jot stuff down on, something that could fit easily into one's pocket to be filed away later. The sticky note does the notecard one better because it's even smaller and easier to carry, and once you've written on one, you can later peel it off and stick it into your receptacle of choice, such as the journal with your project notes in it that is otherwise too awkward to carry around. It is for this reason that I hoard sticky note pads (for some reason, they're kind of expensive) and when a local business is giving them away, I find it excruciatingly difficult to do as the instructions say and "take just one."

Even if you're loath to carry something like a sticky pad on your person, there's always something to write on, cocktail napkins, old envelopes, or, if you're desperate (or, a certain Republican vice-presidential candidate), there's always the palm of your hand. There's also your smartphone, which does have the benefit of fitting in your pocket, as well as a microphone, if you like to speak your notes.

The bottom line is, inspiration can strike at any time, even an inconvenient one. I can't tell you how many times I had to pull my car over to jot something down on a sticky note while I was writing this book. I used to take notes at red lights too, but I stopped after I had a dream that I was broadsided because I ran a red light while doing that. Even though my husband was very understanding about it in the dream, my subconscious mind doesn't need to tell me anything twice.

At any rate, this receptacle, whether it's a journal full of sticky notes, your palm, or your smartphone, comes in handy when you sit down to your desk, because at that point it's only a matter of dipping back into that well you've been filling all along and seeing what comes up.

Self-challenges

Another way to keep the ink flowing is by participating in writing challenges, alone or with others. As a prose writer, one of my favorites is NaNoWriMo, or National Novel Writing Month, a website and organization that supports you extensively as you challenge yourself to write a 50,000 word novel in a month, usually in November. There are also various other challenges, such as the "Poem A Day" challenge in April, which is National Poetry Month, and National Nonfiction Writing Month (also in November like NaNoWriMo). You name it, there's probably a challenge for it, the key to "challenge" being the writing of a large volume in a short time, a practice which is great for learning the benefit of simply getting the words down and which often leads to creative visions and breakthroughs that cannot happen any other way.

Finally, blogging is also something that can support your creative habit. Maybe you just want to write a post a week about a particular topic, maybe you want to share about your creative process but there's something about the lure of a possible audience that can really light your creative fire. When I started blogging about writing and teaching ten years ago, I discovered a voice I never knew I had—funny, kind of edgy—and I enjoyed developing it. When I started blogging about writing at the *Huffington Post*, the audience that venue provided excited me on a whole new level. Realizing how much I had to say about the subject and that people were actually listening led directly to the birth of this book.

Bribes and other psychological techniques

As a curious person in the early twenty-first century, I am fairly easily distractable and as I have mentioned earlier, I have to set up all kinds of barriers to prevent myself from wandering off into cyberspace to read the next fascinating essay or story. But I also advocate the good bribe. Along these lines: I am a huge coffee lover but I only allow myself this beverage when I am actually working on my writing—if I'm still procrastinating, reading social media posts or literary gossip then there will be no coffee for me—even if it means the contents of the cup beside me is turning cold. This practice has the dual benefit of forcing me to get down to business and setting up a pretty solid association in my brain between the act of writing and my favorite warm substance coursing through my veins. But you get the idea—do whatever you can to reward yourself either while you're writing or right afterwards, with something you enjoy. It helps to keep you focused.

Finding sustained time: Get thee to a writers' colony

Most of the writing I've talked about here is the kind that happens in regular one- or two-hour bursts, with perhaps a few longer sessions thrown in weekly or monthly. This book isn't really for those rare unicorn writers who manage to make a living at it full time. Besides, I've always felt that good, solid work could be produced that way, in regular, short bursts.

When I finished my first novel, *The Lost Son*, however, I found that the first draft felt choppy and uneven. As I revised and rewrote that draft, I began to feel that what I really needed was a long, uninterrupted period in which to live in the world of the novel. I needed some time at a writers' colony.

Fortunately, there's a great writers' retreat just three hours from where I live, the Writers' Colony at Dairy Hollow in Eureka Springs,

Arkansas. Founded by cookbook and children's book author Crescent Dragonwagon, Dairy Hollow is a good residency to start with. It's not as competitive as some to get into (like Yaddo or Millay) and it's a reasonably priced (subsidized), idyllic spot to get a lot of work done. For far less than the cost of a sterile hotel room and with all meals included, you get a homey room nestled in the Ozarks, the company of other writers (if you wish) and large swaths of uninterrupted time to devote to your work.

I was only at Dairy Hollow for one week and it still transformed my writing life. I've always been productive, but I never thought I was one of those writers who could write more than a couple of hours a day (truth be told, I can't think of anything I can do more than a couple of hours a day; I like to change things up). Turns out, given the right circumstances, I can. In order to make the narrative more even and consistent, I decided to re-write the entire novel during my stay, which required several seven- to ten-hour writing days. It was nothing short of revelatory to experience this new kind of creative rhythm and to know that it was possible. There is something transformative about being in a place entirely devoted to making it possible for you to write—from providing you meals to leaving you pretty much alone with your thoughts and your words, in a place removed from the whirr and noise of civilization. My digs were more than comfortable, but I noticed the first morning of my stay that the mirror in the bathroom was hung on the wall almost six inches above my head. I may be fairly petite, but still, being unable to see myself in a mirror even on tiptoes sent a pretty clear message. It doesn't matter what you look like here. It matters what you do. I settled into that routine almost immediately, taking a quick shower and getting right down to work in the mornings with no distractions—no one needing anything from me, no urgent news, bad or good, setting the tone for the day. I even took a few naps and then rolled right back into work, developing a work-sleep-eat cycle that set off a level of creativity I had never tapped into before. Two-hour bursts will probably remain the standard for my regular writing life but my new goal is to fit in some longer writing binges, ideally at a colony, every year.

Coming to the residency experience at middle age, like I did, is later than you need to. I encourage you to start planning for one a year as soon as possible. My recommendation would be to look into colonies that are close to you (there are more than you think; the Appendix lists them) and not as competitive and then, as your accomplishments grow, you can aim for more prestigious and, usually, better subsidized institutions, if you feel so moved.

Wait a minute, you may be thinking. I work a full-time job. How am I going to pull off something like a writing residency? Well, some residencies will allow short stays, like a week—and you do get vacation time, right? And even if a residency isn't on the cards—yet—you can start by fashioning your own residency. Do you have a three-day weekend coming up? Take a fourth day off and head to a quiet place somewhere (sometimes religious retreat houses have openings, sometimes you can just rent a cabin or a hotel room) where you can just focus on a writing project for at least eight to twelve hours in a twenty-four-hour period (more, if you have the stamina). See where it takes you. You may surprise yourself.

Write what only you can write: Or, stalking the competition never works

More than once, I've had the honor of judging writing entries for the Scholastic Art and Writing Awards, a prestigious ninety-year-old program for identifying young artists whose past winners include Truman Capote, Sylvia Plath, and Joyce Carol Oates. I'm pleased to report that the future of American fiction looks bright. Very bright indeed.

Every time, I read writing that takes my breath away. Written by teenagers. And every time I think, "Holy Cow. I wasn't this good at their age. Not even close." I mean, I was already starting to get serious as a writer and to work on my craft, but I was not as good as some of these young people were proving themselves to be on the pages before me. In fact, when I think back on my creative writing courses in college, courses that were filled with very talented people, some of whose names you might even recognize, I'm still somewhat humbled. Because I don't remember any of us writing anything as good as some of the teenagers I have judged.

It's downright daunting to stare down that kind of talent. If you're a writer, it's something you simply have to get used to. Finishing George Saunders' latest short story or Nicole Krauss' most recent novel and thinking, "Well, crap. I wish I'd written that." But the truth is, you can't. No one can. Only George Saunders can write like George Saunders and only Nicole Krauss can write like Nicole Krauss, because a beautiful, brilliant primordial soup of education, experience, reading, nature, and nurture came together to make them the writers they are. Just as it will for you if you trust the process. The only way to succeed as a writer, besides dogged persistence and incredible hard work, is to focus on tapping into your own luminous broth, taking it all the way and finding your subject, the one *only you* can give to the world.

Trust me on this. You have to have faith. Because years will go by while you put in the time, put down the words, all the while thinking, "I wish I could make a sentence that strikes notes like Ann Patchett, or write a paragraph with unadorned intensity of Richard Bausch," or even more likely, rack up the awards or publishing credits or advances of [insert name here] who sat next to you in graduate school or grew up in your home town. Challenging as it is, you can't get caught up in this kind of envy because you simply do not have time for it. None of us do. You must be able to admire the beautiful sentence or the forceful paragraph and be happy for your grad school seat mate or hometown gal (unless they're a jerk, in which case you don't have to be happy, you just have to be patient and wait for karma to make its way around), all the while attending to your own work because if you don't, no one else will. If you don't tell your stories, they won't get told and the world will lose a vital voice it needs to round out the global chorus.

My friend, novelist Tom Williams, put it best when he was speaking to my students and one asked him if he ever got discouraged when he read writers he felt were better than he was. Williams shrugged off the question by explaining that he was already used to dealing with that competition by the time he started writing because he went through college on a basketball scholarship and, in his words, "when you're an athlete, there's always someone better than you."

He speaks the truth. I've been writing for decades, trying on different personas with varying degrees of success, learning, growing. But I've found my groove in the last ten years because I've finally found my voice and my subjects, not by bemoaning or envying the success of others or even competing with them, but by keeping my eyes on my own work, the way our elementary school teachers used to remind us to do. I've written (and continue to write) passionately about the teaching of creative writing, writing that has resulted in five books, including *Rethinking Creative Writing*, which was hailed as both beautifully written and pretty entertaining for a scholarly tome, two qualities that make me enormously proud. I've written two novels that bring to bear my German-American ancestry, my preoccupations with loss, resilience, and love and family history, as well as my experiences as a woman and a citizen of the twenty-first century, on stories *only* I can tell. I am planning a new novel (third in the Queens, NY triptych) and working on a memoir that plumbs those very same depths. *My depths.* And finally, I've been writing this book where I get to give pep talks to my tribe, to the writers who are struggling along with me, as well as the ones who are just starting on their journeys.

If you try to make sure that every time you sit down to write, you have an idea of how you're going to start, if you put in the time and energy and planning and, instead of worrying about the competition, celebrate the fact that someone else is doing wonders with words, wonders that will continue to build a reading and writing future for all of us, you will find that sweet spot too. And it will be all yours.

3

Connecting with readers: Publishing

You are a writer if you write, if you feel called to interpret the world through words, and if you would do this whether or not those words were published. Some of the best writers I have ever known actually don't care if their words ever do get published—some of the best writers I have ever known have never had any eyes on their manuscripts other than their own and for whatever reason, that is how they prefer it. But at a certain point, most writers want to connect with readers. I don't think there's anything wrong with this desire, really, as long as it stems less from ego than it does from the desire to reach someone else, to create an experience as much for them as for yourself or to engage them in such a way that they respond, "Yes, yes me too."

Some would argue with me about the ego factor, that ego and even competition are important in the writing life. But if you've read this far, you know how I feel about that. My feelings are based on nearly thirty years of experience in the literary sphere as a student and a teacher. Anyone I've ever known whose writing was motivated primarily by ego and competition, out of a keen longing to be recognized as the smartest writer in the room, is no longer writing; or if they are, they've never written to the extent they could have. They gave up early or they grew bitter when the accolades didn't come as steadily or at the volume they thought they deserved. They retreated to their corners.

Corners, my friend, are sad places to be.

I don't want that for you and I don't think you want it either. The good news is publishing your writing today, reaching other readers, is both more difficult and easier than ever. Wide open frontiers of self-publishing aside, the rise of the Internet has multiplied the number of publishing outlets exponentially—even as it has made it more difficult to get published work noticed. With the proliferation of websites like Submittable, it's easier than ever to get your work to editors—one of whom you hope will eventually champion it. So as long as you don't set your sights on publishing in the *New Yorker* or *Tin House* right out of the gate or on paying your bills from your early earnings, eventually seeing your work in print is an attainable goal, as is working your way up to more selective outlets. Publishing your work happens over time through a process you can learn and adapt to as you develop as a writer, a process that is no secret and a process that I want to let you in on in this chapter.

First things first

Before you start submitting your work, you need to be absolutely sure that you've committed yourself to learning and developing as a writer—whether through online or face-to-face classes or writing groups and through lots and lots of practice. We talk about finding your community and your people more in later chapters, but it's extremely hard to develop as a writer without some kind of trusted reader—whether that's a teacher, mentor, or writing group—someone who can tell you if your words are hitting their mark and why they may not be. This is an essential part of working on your craft—along with cultivating a drafting and revision process. Final drafts submitted for any publication need to be revised and edited within an inch of their lives, not glanced over once or twice for comma splices. How many drafts you think this will take is up for discussion, but if you're a relatively inexperienced writer, it's probably a lot more than you think. Writing is all about revision. Let me repeat that once more, with feeling, "Writing is all about revision." Revision is where your work develops and where you develop as a writer (remember Alan Cheuse's several hundred thousand words). My drafts undergo anywhere between five and ten significant revisions before they're even close to the submission stage. What's more, I read each draft—whether it's an 800-word essay or a 50,000-word book like this one—out loud in the final stages because, as most writers agree, it's the only way to ensure that the sentences flow well and that you've caught surface errors you will not detect any other way. So make sure you've taken time with your work—time to develop it and time to refine it—before you ask *anyone else* to spend any time with it. Think about it—reading is an *experience*, one in which we agree to give up precious time in order to be transported mentally to another place or frame of mind at the least. Nothing breaks that experience more than imperfect final drafts. Besides, less-than-perfect final drafts won't make it very far. Editors have an overwhelming queue of submissions awaiting their attention. Send them a draft with surface errors and you've simply given them an excuse to move on to the next manuscript in line.

Since other chapters will cover publishing full-length books in depth, we're going to focus here on the process of publishing work in magazines and journals, online and in hard copy, all of which are great steps toward publishing longer work, if that's a direction you want to head. Again, building a writing and publishing career is a marathon, not a sprint, and publishers and agents like to see that you've done a lot of 5 and 10ks before you set out to publish your book. In other words, they want to see that you've been distance training for some time and you're serious about this work.

Connect locally, regionally: Start small and build

While you're finding your people, spending time supporting the arts and other writers in your local and online community, going to readings and book launches, haunting independent bookstores, keep your ears open for immediate local publishing opportunities. Here's where you'll find out that the state arts magazine is looking to diversify into publishing poetry and fiction, or that the local interest magazine needs a book reviewer—and a publishing credit is a publishing credit, it all goes toward building your credibility and your career and ultimately, connecting with other readers. Establish yourself as that book reviewer who knows what she's talking about and who knows, maybe the editor of the literary review of the university in town might start wondering if you've got any fiction or poetry to submit.

Know what's going on in literary culture: Read, read, read

You need to stay abreast of and support literary culture if you want to publish in it. If you haven't done this already, find a handful of journals and literary magazines that represent the work in the genre you aspire to, subscribe to them and read them regularly. Check in with the websites of these journals on a weekly basis. Subscribe to the many free reviews and newsletters that cater to the kind of work you want to write and publish and read them, daily or weekly. If this is really the life you want, this should be a happy burden, a reward. As a literary writer, I read the *New York Times Book Review* weekly (and listen to their podcast) and the online aggregator Literary Hub (lithub.com) daily (I also subscribe to the *New York Times*, the *Washington Post*, and *The Guardian* digitally, paying special attention to media news) as well as anything published by industry specialist Jane Friedman, including her speciality biweekly e-newsletter, *The Hot Sheet*. I also read *Literary Mama* (online), the *Oxford American*, the *Rumpus* (online), *Salon* (online), and the *New Yorker*—on the whole, a relatively thin slice of the magazines and journals published today. Still, you may wonder how I have time to do this—and it is a valid question—although keep in mind that in the literary world, a lot of people read even more than that. As a passionately curious person, I could spend literally all day just keeping up with the news of the world, news of the writing world specifically. So I spread my reading out in increments over the course of the day as a reward for finishing less-than-scintillating tasks. For example, after work on that grant budget, I will see what's new today on the Literary Hub and allow myself to read a choice essay. On Fridays, after I've completed my word count for the day, I'll spend some time with a cup of coffee and the *New York Times Book Review* before I begin other work. *The Hot Sheet* will sit in my inbox as a reward for reading five student essays. Spreading tasks out, whether writing or exercise or folding laundry, has always worked for me—but you might have a different system. Maybe you'll spend several hours on Saturday catching up on literary news all at once or read from a literary journal each morning before you start your day—whatever it is, you need to cultivate a reading practice, like writing, and you need to make being a part of the literary world a conscious act.

It also goes without saying that you need to read books—both the classics and those being published today. You need to read excessively, compulsively, as much or more than you write. I'm assuming you've been an inveterate reader your whole life but if you haven't been, you have a lot of catching up to do. You can learn a great deal in writing classrooms and from other writers, but by far the most comprehensive and effective education a writer can ever receive is that which he receives from reading the work of other writers and letting it penetrate his consciousness on a liminal and subliminal level. I am still surprised to find traces of influence from books that I read decades ago—such as *A Tree Grows In Brooklyn*—emerging in my own work. Reading is like filling a well with rich, nourishing water you can dip into whenever you write—a deep well filled with every word, every sentence rhythm you've ever absorbed swirling around in there waiting to be pulled up by your particular bucket. You want your bucket to plummet to the depths, not to bounce around half empty at the surface.

Cast a wide net, work your way up; thicken your skin

Once you've developed your craft and revised until your eyeballs bleed, you're ready to start submitting your work. If you've been committed to the practice of reading and knowing what's going on in the literary world, hopefully you've begun to envision a list of outlets that publish the kinds of work you write. That's a good place to start. But it's important to add to that list by routinely skimming and subscribing to calls for submissions at sites like *NewPages*, *Duotrope*, *Aerogramme Writers*, *Submishmash* (by Submittable), the CRWROPPS LISTSERV, and in the U.S., in the classified sections of *Poets and Writers* magazine and the Association of Writers and Writing Programs' *Chronicle*, which regularly list open calls for submissions (a complete list of these outlets and their websites can be found in the Appendix). Here's what's important about these sections: Most publications are overrun with submissions, far more than they can print. However, at least publications that advertise for submissions are actively seeking them out—they haven't been utterly buried by manuscripts yet, or they wouldn't be advertising.

Once you read about a publication that sounds interesting in one of these classifieds, do a little more research. Look at their website. See if you can read a sample publication or two or at least some samples of what they publish or a mission statement to get a sense if you write what they're looking for. Do your homework. There's no point in submitting a memoir piece about learning to bake from your grandmother to an edgy magazine defined by surrealism in the South. If there does seem to be a fit, add them to your growing list of places to send your work. And then SEND IT OUT. Multiple times. Multiple copies.

Most submitting these days is done online through Submittable, or at least through email. Just thank your lucky stars that you didn't come of age in the days when you had to send your work out in manila envelopes at $1–2 in postage (not to mention the cost of the copy and the human power to put it all together). It's much easier to submit work now. Which is a good thing because you want to submit your well-targeted work as much *as possible*.

Translated, this means submitting your work simultaneously unless a magazine or journal tells you otherwise. As I said, most outlets are swamped with submissions and most editors work for free or for very little money, doing full-time work on the side. It takes them a long time—often many months—to get through that virtual submission pile. What's more, it takes the average manuscript at least *ten* tries before it finds a home. Given those statistics, if you *didn't* simultaneously submit, you'd be old and gray before you published anything. Most editors understand this. Just be sure, if your work is accepted at one publication, to let the others know right away (or, on Submittable, to withdraw your submission) so they don't waste their time considering it.

This statistic is also why you need to submit often and you need to develop a thick skin against rejection. Writing is a subjective art. What one editor might like another might hate, or have already seen ten times in their particular virtual slush pile that week. You've got to keep at it and keep sending your work out. You can't take these rejections too personally if you want to eventually find that editor who will love your writing and be excited to publish it.

Cover letters: Any kind of submission (even those on Submittable) needs to come with a very brief cover letter explaining what it is you are sending, and providing a similarly brief biography (two–four sentences) demonstrating your commitment as a writer—either through your other publications, your academic qualifications, or your appreciation of that publication in particular—and that you have researched the market and done your homework. Editors get all kinds of weird submissions, from stories written in orange crayon on prison stationery to hastily composed drivel that suggests the author only took up writing last Thursday, so a professional cover letter will show them that you are serious and that your writing is at least worth a look. Over time, as you gather more and more publications, starting out with the local arts paper and moving on to several mid-range journals, you will show editors that your work is even more worthy of a read based on the other publications you have.

The other good thing about sending out simultaneous submissions is that this practice will inevitably help you to deal better with rejection. If you only send out one or two precious manuscripts, you pin all your hopes on them, their fates becoming far too dear when you consider that they're still something that an editor might pick up to read after a sleepless night with a colicky baby or upon receipt of a huge tax bill. When you get that one or two—and only one or two—rejections on the manuscript that has borne all your hopes and dreams, you may be crushed. So crushed it will be difficult to muster the strength to send out some more. On the contrary, if you have a large number of manuscripts circulating at any one time, you not only increase the odds that one will be picked up but you decrease the odds that *you* will be destroyed by one rejection. Rejection will become commonplace, which is just as it should be.

Let me say that again. Rejection will become commonplace. Rejection *should* become commonplace.

Interpreting rejection

Rejections tend to be what is known in the literary world as "tiered." That is, if your work didn't really strike a chord, you may just get a quick, canned response saying thanks but no thanks. If an editor liked what she saw but didn't love the piece or perhaps had a few issues with it that were deal breakers, she might write back with something along the lines of, "thanks, try us again next time." This is a hopeful sign. An even more hopeful sign is when an editor addresses you personally and lets you know that if you made some changes to your manuscript, they would consider publishing it, otherwise known as a "revise and resubmit." As long as these changes fit your vision for the work, you should always give the "revise and resubmit" your best effort. Think about it—an editor, who is generally swamped with so many submissions they can barely see straight, thinks so highly of your manuscript that they have taken the time to give you feedback on how you can make it something they will want to publish. This is an exceedingly rare opportunity. Don't let it slip away.

Narrowing the field: Anthologies and themed issues

One way to break into publishing is to narrow the field and keep your eye out for calls for anthologies and themed issues of journals. Let me try to explain this to you visually. I am 5′3″ tall, which is about the height of the virtual slush pile of submissions at most magazines and journals if it were to be printed out and stacked top to bottom: Work that has come in over the transom, unsolicited. Now, imagine what the pile might be like for manuscripts about "love and sex in your 40s" or essays "that explore the subject of women who have served as mother-surrogates for other people's children (i.e. aunts, nannies, and so forth). The pile shrinks considerably, rising perhaps only to my ankle or mid-calf. Because not nearly so many people have work about "love and sex in your 40s" or whatever the topic on their hard drive, but if you happen to have something lying around that fits that subject perfectly, your competition has suddenly evaporated. By the way, both of these examples are real cases of anthologies I discovered in the *Poets and Writers* classified section and actually published in, because I'd already been planning to write about these subjects anyway and I knew the odds of acceptance were high. The same goes for "themed issues" of journals— say an upcoming issue of your favorite journal is looking for poetry about food—and you just happen to have a sonnet series about veganism—submit! Because their submissions pile (virtual or otherwise) for this issue is going to be a great deal smaller than it would be for an unthemed issue, significantly raising your chances of acceptance.

Writing contests

There are a number of valid reasons why a writer might become a "professional writing contest entrant": Doing so is one way (especially for poets whose prospects with commercial houses are more limited) to break into publishing through smaller houses when the big houses dominate the market with more commercial fare. Others argue that paying contest fees amounts to a kind of literary citizenship wherein we all pay a sort of "dues" to keep these small houses and literary magazines afloat. I don't disagree; in fact, I just sent a $30 reading fee for my novel off to a contest today. So yes, even I occasionally succumb to the hope that my novel might get plucked from the contest slush.

But can you really beat the odds? Some industry insiders seem to think that simply by submitting to a large number of contests, a writer with a high-quality manuscript will eventually prevail. Based on my experience as a judge for some of these competitions, I'm not so sure.

It was my first experience as a screening judge for a writing contest in graduate school that really opened my eyes. Now, let me be clear, this contest and the others I have since been a part of, are fair, ethical competitions, nothing like those that Foetry.com and *Poets and Writers'* "The Contester" column exposed some years back, when they revealed that several well-known contests were heavily weighted toward students and/or friends of the final judges. But contests can be more of the crapshoot than one might think, and not always one I'm willing to pay for.

Twenty years ago, in the conference room of the English Department at the University of Louisiana-Lafayette, I gathered with nine other graduate student screeners to receive my first stack of fiction entries. Each of us would bring home ten manuscripts and return a few days later with the one manuscript from our pile we believed should go forward to the final "celebrity" judge.

I took my job very seriously, as did the other first-round judges I'm sure, carefully reading and re-reading each manuscript and comparing it to the others. More than half of the stories had issues that eliminated them from the race early on but ultimately, it came down to two or three quality manuscripts. Looking back, the final decision was agonizing.

Then it dawned on me, once we reassembled in that conference room, redolent of the department chair's cigarette smoke and the sweat of many a nervous student writer who'd once been on the workshop hot seat, that the choices we had all made were highly subjective. I felt pretty good about my decision until I looked around at my fellow grad student judges and realized that, while we all might have narrowed it down to the same two or three, some of them would have made a different final selection from my pile.

We were as disparate as a roomful of people could be, with markedly diverse aesthetic tastes. Some of us were in a punk band. Others would never be cool enough to be in a punk band (yours truly). Some were going through a magical realism phase. Others worshiped Ken Kesey and the Merry Pranksters and had begun to believe the government was tapping their phone. I wondered, "How would a manuscript of mine [at the time I was and still am a fairly mainstream literary realist] fare in this room?"

Since then, I've never been able to enter a writing contest without calling to mind that motley Star Chamber. Sure, whenever you submit something to a publication, it's going have to pass through one or two graduate students or editorial assistants at the gate. But at least when I submit to a journal, I've researched the publication well enough to know if my work is at least in the ballpark of what they tend to publish.

Sometimes I write the check anyway, deciding that supporting the contest, the press, or the journal is more important. But I keep my eye out for free contests. Yes, balance is important and so is supporting the arts, which is why our household subscribes to more than our fair share of literary magazines (between my husband and me, it contains more than its fair share of writers). I recommend my students do the same. If you're going to submit to literary magazines, you owe it to them to subscribe to some, even in your salad days. Besides, it's the only way to truly immerse yourself in the literary culture of your generation. But when it comes to contests, be judicious. If you enter a fee-based contest, do it as much as because you want to support that particular literary endeavor as anything else. And when you find a no-fee contest jump on it. Always. After all, you have nothing to lose.

Be thankful

One final word, or rather, three words: thank you notes. Your mother was right. Send them. You need to send one for every response you get to your writing, even to generic rejections. First of all, once you start to submit a high volume of work, you'll learn that some editors don't even acknowledge your submission with a rejection— your submissions will disappear into the ether, never to be heard from again (although feel free to follow through and check on them), which will make you particularly grateful for editors who *do* take the time to let you know how your work fared with them. Editors work hard— usually for low pay, often for free—and they deserve some appreciation. Also, thanking them gives you one more chance to get your name in front of them in a positive way, so that the next time they get a submission from you they'll be favorably inclined from the get-go: "Oh look, another piece from that kind Jane Writer, who is always so appreciative of my time." It won't take long—just a quick email reply thanking the editor for her efforts. And just think how happy it will make your mother, too.

4

Writing geeks unite: Finding your tribe

In "Six Degrees of Lois Weisberg," the landmark 1999 *New Yorker* article later reprinted in his book *The Tipping Point*, Malcolm Gladwell offers this Chicago cultural diva as the epitome of a "connector," someone whose unique personality brings many people across different social strata together. Along those same lines, I can't remember whether I met poet and essayist Anna Leahy because Kelly Ritter and I published her essay in our first collection, *Can It Really be Taught?: Resisting Lore in Creative Writing Pedagogy*, or because she and I worked together leading a national writing conference teaching forum. Both events happened around the same time, so it's a chicken and egg situation. She would probably know, because Anna knows everything. And everyone. Really. An alumni of the famed undergraduate writing program at Knox College, where she first began cultivating her tribe, as well as a graduate of an MA, an MFA, and a Ph.D. program, Anna's connections are legion, not because she went to a lot of schools and knows a lot of people but because she is truly a portrait of the kind of curiosity, sociability, and energy that Gladwell describes. She is always proposing a new project for us to work on together (and, in keeping with her status of "connector," I am just one of the many people and projects she is usually working with) or introducing me to someone I haven't met or something I haven't read yet but must. I count myself as extremely lucky to be part of Anna's capacious circle.

I do give myself some credit for reaching out to Anna, the same way I did with my former longtime collaborator, Kelly Ritter, or with the late Wendy Bishop or UK creative writing guru Graeme Harper. I put myself out there. In the last two cases, I wrote to these field leaders and introduced myself to them, expressing my admiration for their work. I looked for ways for us to work together. Sometimes you have to do that in writing and in life. Much as those of us who wave the introvert flag would like to believe otherwise, that we can just hunker down, do the work, send it out and wait for the royalty checks to come flooding back, in today's literary landscape that just isn't the reality. Sometimes you have to look beyond yourself and practice what's become known as "literary citizenship." Writer Cathy Day, a champion of literary citizenship who even teaches a class on the subject, frames it this way:

> Lately, I've started thinking that maybe the reason I teach creative writing isn't just to create writers, but also to create a populace that cares about reading. There are many ways to lead a literary life, and I try to show my students simple ways that they can practice what I call "literary citizenship." I wish more aspiring writers would contribute to, not just expect things from, that world they want so much to be a part of.[1]

Here's the thing: A side benefit of contributing to that world is that you start to cultivate your own tribe. You surround yourself with people who care about the same things you do, not about finding new ways to make or spend money, for example, but about how to create art and support it. Anyone pursuing a writing life needs the company of this kind of tribe to keep going during the lean months, months that sometimes turn into years. But sometimes they also find, as I have, that by practicing literary citizenship they fertilize the landscape that surrounds them, so that when the seeds of opportunity float down they are far more likely to take root.

Anna's success as a poet, essayist, and as the literary world's Lois Weinberg is also notable for one thing she's not: Anna is not a mean girl. I assume there are some mean girls (and guys) in the creative writing world (because, alas, such people seem to exist in every sphere), but fortunately I don't know many of them personally. We know their kind, though, the kind who achieve success by shutting out a lot of other people along the way. Give these people a wide berth in your writing life and, for God's sake, don't become one of them. Paul McCartney was right: In the writing world as in life, the love you take really is equal to the love you make. Fill your tribe with other writers who are generous and kind to one other, treat them the same way, work with them to make a world where the "word" is cherished and the rewards of a writing life rich with friendship, support—and opportunity will follow.

That's all well and good, you may be thinking, but before we all join hands for a rousing chorus of Kumbaya, how, exactly do I do this?

Reach out

One of the main ways to connect to other writers and to find your tribe is to do what you've been told to do since nursery school: Use your words, or write to them. Back in the day, this meant writing snail mail letters of appreciation to writers whose work you admired (writer Carolyn See calls these "charming notes" in her wonderful book *Making a Literary Life*). When you finish reading a book or an essay or a poem you love, dash off a quick note or email to the author and tell them. Writers love this; we live for these little nods of appreciation or understanding, in fact, it's one reason many of us write.

What do you have to lose? Either the writer responds and you have a nice conversation and make a connection—or they don't and you move on. I've made so many online friendships this way, simply by contacting the author of something I read and telling them how deeply their work affected me, friendships that have significantly expanded my literary community far beyond the "fly-over" state that I live in. Friendships that have benefited me and even my students as I join different networks of writers in different genres and social media venues.

Another case in point: I had a friend we'll call Joe who made it a point to write to every author whose book he'd read and admired, personalizing his contact perhaps with a question about the book or an example of how it had affected him. For example, after reading Kim Stafford's *The Muses Among Us: Eloquent Listening and Other Pleasures of the Writer's Craft*, Joe wrote Stafford and included in his message the results of one of Stafford's assignments to "write a hundred-word sentence." In fact, Stafford was very taken with Joe's sentence and ended up passing it along to an editor friend of his who was looking for flash fiction for his journal. You can guess how that turned out.

Do be careful here. Refrain from including any requests with these contacts—requests such as: "I loved the last book in your trilogy; now would you be willing to read and comment on my 100,000-word novel on beekeeping in the twenty-fourth century?" Writers are as overworked as anyone and get these kind of requests all the time, besides. Keep the connection strictly based on your admiration for their work. And try not to "fangirl" or "fanboy" too much—be mature about your expression and focus on describing specifically what impacted you, rather than the fact that you think the object of your affection is the "best writer ever." Allow normal communications to take place.

Attend readings and literary events in your area

Going to readings and literary events in your area is probably the best way to start meeting other people like you, people with an appreciation for the written word. How do you find out about these events? Keep your eye out: Bookstores, libraries, and coffee shops frequently post them, as do local universities. Most of these institutions will have email or snail mail newsletters. Make sure you get on their address lists to find out about the latest events. Attend as many as you can to support other writers. Try to notice people you see regularly and strike up a conversation. Find out what their literary interests are and if you have anything in common. Ask them if they know of any other literary events happening you can support or of any literary societies or writing clubs you can join. Sometimes specific genres even have regional clubs, such as the local chapter of the Society for Children's Book Writers and Illustrators, which often runs local writing conferences as well. If there are large-scale events, like conferences and book festivals, offer yourself to the organizers as a volunteer as a way of getting involved.

If the number of literary events scheduled in your area seems particularly slim to nonexistent, consider it an opportunity to get something started, like an open mic reading night once a week at a local café.

Form or join a writing group

Forming a writing group is another way to make inroads into literary culture in your area while developing your craft at the same time. First, consider asking around at the readings that you're attending:

"Are there any local writing groups around here that are open to new members?" If the answer is no, consider asking if anyone at these readings might be interested in forming such a group. Failing that, put some posters up at the libraries, bookstores, and coffee houses that you frequent, advertising the formation of a writing group with an informational meeting. Finally, if you live in an extremely rural area, consider joining an online writing group such as Figment or The Next Big Writer.

Found a literary magazine or press

With the growth of publishing-on-demand, founding a literary magazine requires less overhead than ever before. Perhaps you feel a kinship with some of the members of the your writing group and some of you would like to support the literary arts by promoting new work in a magazine—or maybe you even want to take on this task alone. Take some online publishing courses, teach yourself the latest publishing software, put the call out for new work and take the plunge. There are so many advantages to taking this approach. You'll be celebrating new writing, learning how to publish and promote the work of other writers as well as defining your own aesthetic philosophy as you read submissions, which can only enhance your own literary development. In a small but significant way, you'll be joining a publishing community where you can learn about other local and regional publications and benefit from being part of a larger network of people promoting the written word.

You're probably noticing a theme here—seek out your people in your local area and if you can't find opportunities to promote the literary culture you love, create them. Ralph and Margot Treitel didn't wait for the literary world to come to them in Columbia,

Maryland, in the 1970s, even though they were busy people with jobs and a family: They made their own, leaving an artistic legacy that remains to this day.

Note

1 Day, Cathy. "What's Literary Citizenship?" http://thebooksistah.com/ authorsite/whats-literary-citizenship/

5

Continuing your education: What makes sense for you?

No one is simply born a writer but comes to this place through a long apprenticeship or education. You can approach this education by attending a series of writing courses at educational institutions, earning a Bachelor of Arts to a Master of Arts or a Master of Fine Arts or even a Ph.D. (or their equivalents at institutions in the UK or other countries) that will lead you through a process of development as a writer including reading, discussion, instruction, instructor feedback, peer feedback, and sustained writing. Or, you can approach this education as an intensely personal one outside of formal education institutions, one focused on dedicated reading, reflection, and practice—the act of doing the writing itself. You can also do some of both as you develop as a writer, pursuing education during those times when it makes sense and going the self-didactic route when you have the time and the energy to motivate yourself. Let me guide you through some approaches to hastening your development as a writer:

Undergraduate programs

My own bias aside (I've taught in an undergraduate writing program, which I helped found, for two decades), if you're just setting out to pursue a college degree and are particularly interested in writing, an undergraduate writing major can be excellent preparation for people who want to lead writing lives that include working in editing, publishing, arts management, advertising, and Web development. Look for programs that include courses in creative writing as well as courses in editing, publishing, and writing for digital media, as well as internships—an undergraduate major should necessarily be more general as students in an undergraduate program haven't necessarily decided how or whether to specialize yet. My students go on to find wonderful jobs in advertising, digital media, Web design and content, and so forth which provide them with satisfying livelihoods while they pursue their creative writing. Some decide to specialize further with MFAs and Ph.D.s. And some have even published books with independent presses—with just the undergraduate degree. Shameless plug here, however, as with any undergraduate program, you should be savvy about how you proceed through your course of study. I have edited a book called *Studying Creative Writing Successfully* that provides a guide to doing just that, with essays from how to get the most out of a creative workshop class to preparing yourself to get a job after you graduate. If you've already achieved an undergraduate degree in something else, however, you don't need to go back to school to pick up an undergraduate writing degree unless you want to make a career change that includes editing and publishing and even in that case, you would probably do well to simply get a certificate or additional training in the courses you need for those kinds of positions. You will most likely benefit from creative writing classes to enhance your development, however, and from considering at least one of the courses of study below.

Master of Fine Arts and Master of Arts programs

Do I believe the Master of Fine Arts degree in writing can help writers? Absolutely. I've spent the last ten years researching these programs in the U.S. and abroad, ultimately writing a book, *Rethinking Creative Writing Programs: Programs and Practices That Work*. I'm also a big fan of the work of Mark McGurl, whose book *The Program Era: Postwar Fiction and the Rise of Creative Writing* revealed that the emergence of these programs has had a significant effect on the growth of American literature in the last seventy-odd years. Finally, I have the degree myself, from George Mason University, with a specialization in fiction writing.

For proof that the Master of Fine Arts in writing is a degree that has been hotly debated for decades, we need look no further than Iowa Writers' Workshop alum Flannery O'Connor's famous remark that far from producing too many writers, universities did not discourage enough of them. After over a decade studying what has been written about the degree, I've concluded that there will always be those who say that creative writing can't or shouldn't be taught, that the programs are rife with teachers who promote generic McStories and McPoems and who lack an understanding of the publishing world, and that the classes themselves are filled with mawkish students interested only in the therapeutic value of self-expression. It's simply too easy an accusation to make and the writers/teachers in the programs are often too busy teaching and writing to defend themselves. I do think there's ample room for improvement—that's what my book is about—but I also think that we're starting to see programs evolve beyond a curriculum that revolves completely around the workshop.

But back to the MFA itself. Here's what I tell my students.

An MFA program can:

- Give you time and support to focus on your craft and thus accelerate your development as a writer.

- Provide you with advice and teaching from published writers (and visiting writers) who, if you've selected your program well, are successful in the kind of writing *you* want to do.

- Surround you with peers and teachers and visiting writers who care as passionately about the written word as you do.

- Ideally, give you contacts in the publishing world.

- Ideally, if you take the right courses and consciously pursue the right opportunities in a program that best fits your interests, help you break into an editorial career in literary publishing, new media, or another writing-related career that hasn't been invented yet (publishing is changing that quickly).

- Ideally, if you take the right courses (in pedagogy), publish significantly, or consider further degrees (Ph.D.), this will help you pursue a job in teaching writing (if that's what you're passionate about).

An MFA program *cannot*:

- Lead directly to a cushy job teaching creative writing or to a wildly successful publishing career à la Stephen King or J. K. Rowling (neither of whom attended one, anyway).

If you want to apply:

- Read widely in contemporary literature. When you find a writer who feels like a kindred spirit, search the Web and see if this person is teaching anywhere.

- Read Tom Kealey's *The Creative Writing MFA Handbook*. In its second edition, this is the go-to guide on MFA programs. It will help you to find the right program for you and, even more

importantly, help you get the most out of the experience.
I cannot recommend this book strongly enough; in fact, I
recommend it so much you'd think Kealey was giving me
kickbacks.

- Also check out the AWP *Official Guide to Writing Programs*
  and the *Poets and Writers* annual special Fall issue on MFA
  programs as well as their helpful online guide. *Poets and
  Writers* provides a great deal of information about the
  programs themselves, such as cost of living, availability of
  assistantships and fellowships, and so forth. In the quest to
  find the MFA program for you, information is your best ally.
  For that reason, check out the data on NewPages.com as well.

- Once you have narrowed your choices down to a few
  programs, thoroughly research the faculty and the programs
  via their websites. Find out what the faculty have been writing
  and publishing lately. Read a sample. Consider: Is this
  someone I want to work with?

- Try to get a fellowship or an assistantship. Failing that,
  consider strong state programs with lower tuition. Some will
  disagree with me on this point, because there are a number of
  private schools with good programs, a few of which are
  located in cities with a thriving publishing culture, such as
  New York and Boston. But if you can avoid it, you don't want
  to go too deeply in debt for this degree. In fact, try not to go
  into debt at all.

An MFA is also considered a "terminal" degree in the field, which
means that if you have it and you do get that prized teaching job, you
should have the background you need to get tenure and be promoted
at most institutions (so long as you meet the other requirements). An
MA will not certify you for this and you should know that. An MA in

creative writing, because it usually has fewer hours and often, no thesis requirement, is usually considered a first step toward the Ph.D. or to a position teaching secondary public or private school. It will not qualify you to teach at the university level.

Getting an MFA is a highly personal decision. I'm glad I got mine; I would not have had it any other way. It accelerated my development as a writer and was an important step in my career. I teach students who are pursuing one now who don't plan to teach but who do plan to use the degree as a stepping stone to a career in publishing and are well on their way to doing so. Other students have gone on to Ph.D. programs from the MFA and some of my students have used their connections to publish books.

You do not have to get an MFA in order to be a writer. You do have to keep writing, read widely, and continue getting feedback on your writing via an online or face-to-face critique group—that is, you still need to do most of the things I suggest in this book. Don't rule out the possibility of a low-residency MFA program either, especially if you have another career you enjoy but want to continue your writing avocation. I have worked with a number of low-residency MFA programs and have a deep respect for them—they provide a great solution for the writer who wants to accelerate their development and contacts without leaving their current job or location.

One thing to be aware of if you do choose to go for an MFA, is that someone will have an opinion about it. This is in part because education and writing seem to be two issues that everyone always has an opinion about, regardless of how much experience they actually have in it. But it's mainly because the MFA has become a popular thing for people to flout in public in the last twenty years or so, beginning, I think, in the early 80s when Donald Hall called out MFAs for producing McPoems and continuing til this day, to the extent that they have earned their own genre in the literature, what I like to call the "MFA Think Piece." While I have never written such a piece, I have read many of them, so many in fact, that I have developed my own set of instructions for anyone who is thinking of writing them. I encourage you to read them—as you would any think piece you will no doubt come across—with a grain of salt and form your own opinions.

How to write an MFA think piece: A brief introduction to the genre

Are you thinking of writing a detailed, critical response to your experience with an MFA program—studying in one or teaching in one? Maybe you've just read about the phenomena and decided—what the hell, I'll throw in my two cents. Or, maybe you're considering pursuing one of these advanced degrees in creative writing and find the online debate about them intriguing.

Perhaps these guidelines will help.

First and foremost, with the exception of the one or two essays you might reference, avoid the Internet. I cannot emphasize this enough. Specifically, take care to construct your argument as if Google had never been invented and the search terms "creative writing," "creative writing programs," and "higher education" existed utterly outside your lexicon. In order to maintain this illusion, in fact, it might be best to pretend it's still 1996. Listen to Mariah Carey, Boyz II Men, and Alanis Morissette. Watch *Seinfeld* and *Frasier* reruns. Do the macarena.

Second, but perhaps just as important, if your experience has been with a famous, iconic MFA program, such as at the University of Iowa, the University of Michigan, New York University, Syracuse University, or similar, don't worry; it is less incumbent on you to investigate what is going on at the other programs, as it is a fact generally accepted in US culture that whatever is going on in those programs represents whatever is happening at the literally hundreds of full-residency or low-residency programs across the nation. Nonetheless, feel free to extrapolate from your own personal silo of knowledge. If your program was short on literary history and professional preparation, most likely the other 300-plus programs are as well and it's safe to assume that prescribing a "new MFA" that is more thorough in these areas will solve those problems. This is especially true if your MFA is more than five years old. We all know the MFA does not change much. The "we" here is universal, by the way, no need to credit sources, even if you invoke the need for more literary study in your critique (heads up if you go that route though—literary scholars are notoriously picky about the whole sources thing—they call them "lit reviews"). And if a critic or reviewer does call you out on the fact that you neglected to contextualize your own argument, just tell them that you didn't have time to do the research. Really. Nobody has time for that.

If you're going to take this all the way, make certain not to attend the annual AWP (Association of Writers and Writing Programs) Conference, where you might inadvertently walk into a session on innovation in creative writing programs, teaching, or the workshop. If you do end up attending (say the conference is in your home city or something) and this does happen accidentally, leave the session immediately lest you begin to receive confusing signals that conflict with your worldview. Go back into the hallway and re-check the program for the session on publishing you were actually looking for or return to the book fair for another round of networking (making sure your name tag is clearly visible).

But what was that thing that guy in the beard at the front of the room said as you were walking out? Something about the "Global MFA?" What even *is* a "Global MFA?"

Great. The publishing panel you were heading for is standing room only and there doesn't seem to be anyone who can do anything for you at the book fair right now. Maybe you should take a load off and try to figure out what that last session was all about. Especially since there were still a few open seats in the back.

So it turns out "Innovations in the MFA program" was the name of the session you just left. Apparently innovation in creative writing programs has been, like, a "thing" in the last decade or so. Who knew? MFAs in New Media at the University of Missouri-Kansas City, Global MFAs at the University of Nevada-Las Vegas, MFAs in Comics at the California College of the Arts. MFAs built on teaching presses like the ones at the University of North Carolina-Wilmington, the University of New Orleans, and Augsburg College.

It turns out that this MFA panel is part of a whole pedagogy "strand," at the conference, with sessions on alternatives to the workshop, grading creative writing, teaching genre fiction and, well, dozens of others. You begin to wonder if this whole idea of creative writing pedagogy has just sprung up suddenly—after all, you've never heard of it before today—or if its been building for a while.

You lift the Google ban and try those very search terms. Creative writing in higher education. Creative writing pedagogy. Ok then. These people have been busy—how do they have time to do this, write all this stuff about teaching creative writing *and* do their own creative writing? Binge-watching *True Detective* must be off the list.

Holy cow, some of these people have been doing this for almost twenty years! A few of the names come up over and over. This Wendy Bishop, for example, she's all over the place. Wendy Bishop. Wendy Bishop. Wendy Bishop—a one-woman writing machine. And then she disappears—and it's more hit or miss. Dianne Donnelly, Pat Bizzaro (how's that for a name), Kelly Ritter, Anna Leahy, Tim Mayers, Graeme Harper, Mark McGurl. People from the UK and Australia. Books, like

Does the Workshop Still Work? What We Talk About When We Talk About Creative Writing. Can It Really Be Taught? Rethinking Creative Writing. Creative Writing and the Digital Age. You'd think this was a movement or something. But if it was a movement . . .

Oh. Right. There is a website. The Creative Writing Studies Organization. Creativewritingstudies.com.

Seriously though, your head is about to EXPLODE. You had a really good essay going until now, just exploring, *really interrogating,* your own experience. For example, here's an idea. Didn't a famous writer—you think it was even a woman—once say that the problem with creative writing programs was that they didn't stifle enough creative writers? You are *sure* you heard that somewhere. You could look it up but you've decided to swear off Google again—it's nothing but trouble. You didn't go into almost six figures worth of debt studying with famous writers for nothing. People should take your word for it. And cutting back on all those programs would be a place to start. Do they really need every single one? There should be a quota on writers! Or some of these programs should become more rigorous! Add more literature courses! Courses where you have to look stuff up! At least, the people in *those* programs should! What are students even doing in those places? I don't actually know, to tell you the truth, but I know what they should be doing. Getting back to basics!

Ph.D. programs

It wasn't long after I stepped into the classroom twenty-five years ago, as a teaching assistant in the George Mason University MFA Program, that I realized I wanted to teach. I loved being in a classroom with college students, even though at the time most of them were only a few years younger than I was (and one of them, a retired Coast

Guardsman I'll never forget, named Art Owen, was twice my age). I loved spending my days writing, reading, or talking about writing with my composition students. When I graduated, however, the job pickings for a thinly published young MFA graduate on the advanced-degree-saturated East coast were slim and the Ph.D. option began to hold more appeal.

To be honest, my husband and I looked into our Ph.D. program at the University of Louisiana at Lafayette rather casually; it was the only program we applied to that year, in part because at the time, the application cost only five dollars. If we got their coveted fellowship, it seemed like an excellent way to spend three more years writing and pick up another degree at the same time. If we didn't, well, we'd look into some more Ph.D. programs the next year.

And actually, we didn't get any money at first. When the school called to say we'd been accepted but that there were no assistantships or fellowships to spare, we thanked them kindly, said we didn't want to pull up stakes and go into debt at that point and that perhaps we would apply again next year. My husband and I were planning our wedding as well as teaching part-time at our alma mater, George Mason, and working a few other side-hustle jobs between us. I started looking at apartments in Northern Virginia we might be able to afford, if we scrimped (another reason Louisiana had looked good was the significantly lower cost of living).

Then, out of the blue, we got a second call a month later. The University had managed to convince two doctoral fellows to hurry up and graduate and as a result, they were offering us both fellowships. At $12,000 each per year, along with full tuition, no teaching responsibilities (we wanted to teach but we also knew we needed to work on our writing), and subsidized married student housing ($200 per month for two bedrooms, utilities included, which in subtropical Louisiana was a godsend) we felt as if we had won the lottery.

And financially, we certainly had, although over the next three years we would learn that we had also won the lottery in terms of a writing community, in terms of teaching, in terms of mentoring, and in terms of professional support. While our MFA had accelerated our writing development in important ways, our Ph.D. did much more to accelerate our development as academic professionals. We both finished big writing projects—me a novel and my husband a book of short stories— with some of the most attentive mentors we'd ever had; we both filled in significant gaps in our literary knowledge as we read for comprehensive exams that covered all of American literature and several centuries of British, which was also terrific for our writing, and I picked up another field of expertise that seemed tailor-made for me: Composition Theory, which led directly to my research in creative writing studies. We started to publish our work. We developed lifelong mentors and friends, widening our literary community significantly and permanently. We are not unhappy people, my husband and I; at any given time our glasses seem pretty much half-full, but we would probably still tell anyone who asked that those four years at the University of Louisiana-Lafayette were easily some of the best of our lives.

Should you get a Ph.D.? It depends. Do you want to teach? If the answer is yes, unless you've already bagged a couple of published books during your MFA program, it wouldn't hurt. In addition to buying yourself precious time to develop as a writer, you will exponentially deepen your knowledge as a scholar/teacher in ways you can't even imagine yet. But select the right program: One that will support you, with either an assistantship or a fellowship (read: *don't go into debt*) and provide you with mentoring as a writer and as a burgeoning academic professional.

And if you don't want to teach, by all means look for something else to do while you build your writing career. There are plenty of other possibilities but a Ph.D. is probably not for you.

Community schools, workshops, writing centers

As I've mentioned before, it's entirely possible to study writing without pursuing a formal degree and the time commitment that requires. Community schools and writing centers across the country now exist and run a rich number of courses that allow people to do so—and some of them even offer part of their programs online, so you don't need to be located in a certain part of the country in order to avail yourself of them. Taught by experienced, published writers and scheduled at a time when people who work during the day can usually attend, they really constitute a viable alternative. Schools like GrubStreet Writers' Workshop in Boston and Sackett Street Writers' Workshop in New York City offer MFA-level courses, like GrubStreet's twelve-month novel incubator or Sackett Street's twenty-week novel intensive. Graduates of these schools have a great track record for publishing their work and building sustaining writing careers and even though these do offer online courses, so you can take them anywhere, community workshops are springing up all over the country, in places like Eureka Springs, Arkansas, Minneapolis, Minnesota, and Denver, Colorado. A full list of them is available in the Appendix.

Writers' conferences

In addition to community schools, writers' conferences are a great way for aspiring writers to learn more about the field they want to become a part of, both in terms of craft and in terms of professional knowledge. Most states have local and regional conferences where you can take part in workshops that will help you enhance your work, learn more about publishing it, and meet with other people in your region with a passion for writing. These conferences bring in published authors, agents, and publishing professionals to speak and the registration fees are reasonable and well worth their cost.

As you grow as a writer and gather several of these local conferences under your belt, start to consider attending national conferences in your genre. This is where you'll be exposed to even more current craft instruction and where you'll forge even more connections as a writer hoping to grow her career and prospects. As with the community schools, there is a list of the best conferences in the Appendix. I can't emphasize enough that making time for them is a powerful way to learn and grow as a writer and expand your network.

Independent learning

Do you have to do any of these things to succeed as a writer? What if you're a true introvert who never wants to leave her writing desk or interact with other people? I suppose you could hide away, but I think it would be extremely difficult and I don't actually know anyone personally who has. You can and should read as much as possible and well in accelerating your development as a writer, and you should be practicing your writing (remember that gargantuan word count)— you can't succeed without making these acts a part of your practice. But you also need to expose your writing to experienced readers— whether to a teacher, a mentor, a writing group—in order to develop, to learn from their commentary on what works in your poem or story or essay and what does not, and you need to internalize those readerly responses for your next draft. You also need, in the community of other writers, to learn from reading and critiquing the work of your peers. Based on over a quarter-century of experience teaching, I can tell you that reading the work of others and determining how it can be revised to achieve its goals will also accelerate your own development as a writer in ways nothing else can. You can teach yourself a great deal about writing, but you can only learn so much in a vacuum. Even before writing schools existed, artists realized this and developed literary salons and writing groups to provide it. To develop optimally, you need other people, teachers, mentors, honest readers. Seek them out.

6

Making a living: Careers that support the writing life

The starving artist is a myth

When I was a graduate student, iconic writer John Updike came to our university to do a reading. He also asked to speak to the students—something that was not required in his contract and a request that has always struck me as generous of him—and so I had the great good luck of sitting in a molded plastic desk chair while John Updike held forth on the writing life. One of the things he lamented was that due to the changes in publishing it was no longer possible to support oneself entirely through writing. Smiling wistfully, he told us that when he was young, selling a few stories to the *New Yorker* would support his family for a whole year.

That was twenty-five years ago. Since then, publishing has gone through even more drastic changes, meaning that fewer writers than ever support themselves solely through their writing, even by writing books. And when they do begin to support themselves, it's often after years of publishing and building up book sales and backlist sales.

It is for this reason that you must learn to identify yourself as a writer because you write, not because you make a living from your writing. Some writers, especially some of my students, insist that I'm merely being "negative" by telling them this. The first thing you need to know is that I'm actually not a terribly negative person; the second is that in preparing you for reality, I'm not trying to be all doom and gloom. I'm trying to get you ready to make writing your life, so that you can find a way for it to sustain you emotionally—because if you expect it to immediately sustain you financially, the chances are good that you will give up.

And still, to this day, no matter what I say, I have students who tell me that they plan to "write full time," right out of college or encounter people who have just recently taken up writing asking me when they will be able to give up their day jobs. The truth is, you may not be able to give up your day job for a very long time. Perhaps never.

While it's true that very few writers support themselves solely through their writing (and something you need to know up front), that reality doesn't necessarily mean you are going to starve. It does mean you need to plan, however, and it does mean that you need to think hard about your family and lifestyle needs and the extent to which you want the career you have to support your writing to be one that closely *allies* with writing and the literary arts, or whether you might thrive in an entirely different career that draws from different strengths but which enables you to pursue your writing, separately.

Let me explain—because this chapter is really going to focus on careers that closely ally with writing and the literary arts. Some people like to have careers that focus on something completely different from writing, which they view as their *avocation* (defined as an additional occupation pursued along with a primary occupation, normally for passion or pleasure). Historically, great writers have emerged from medicine, insurance, banking—the list goes on—and some of these people *never* gave up their day jobs. Currently, I know of writers who are also speech pathologists, nurses, public relations executives, dietitians, and psychologists. They pursue these careers for a number of different reasons: Because they have other talents and skills they want to exercise, because they discovered writing later in life after they had become well established in another career, because they liked the financial rewards, some of which were higher than if they had pursued careers allied with writing. Often, overwhelmingly, these people chose careers that were quite different from the act of writing because they found that pursuing an allied career in the literary arts drained their brains of the same type of energy they needed to create. In order to preserve that energy, their day jobs needed to focus on different tasks.

This is something for you to think about if you're still considering different career paths. You might try a career in the allied literary arts and see how much energy it leaves for your writing—if it does (I also know loads of writers who are also editors) then you know you're on the right course. If working with words all day leaves you too drained to consider your own, however, you might think about something different to pay the bills.

The rest of this chapter, however, will be devoted to those for whom a day job devoted to words in one way or another, to promoting the literary arts, is the best way they can think of to spend their time and draw a paycheck. I'm one of those people and I also promote these careers for my students—so I can tell you a great deal about the successes my students have had and how they prepared themselves for them. But I can't tell you about all of them—the world is changing too rapidly for that, with new jobs constantly being created that didn't exist five years ago—so *always* be on the lookout for new ways to support yourself through your literary passions.

Editing and publishing

Editing and publishing is an enormous field that encompasses mainstream and independent publishing houses, magazine and online publishing, and literary agenting. Undergraduate degrees in creative writing as well as MFAs in writing can serve as initial stepping stones to jobs in this field; internships are also extremely important. Fortunately, some of these can now be done virtually, so you can do an internship for a literary magazine in Chicago while attending school in Kansas City. As you can imagine, you want to plan and prepare for these types of positions. While an undergraduate or graduate student, make sure that in addition to workshop and craft classes, you also take courses in editing, publishing, and information design. Try to get on the staff of the campus literary journal and learn how the nuts and bolts of publication works. Finally, aim for at least one, ideally two or even three, internships while you're an undergraduate—either for course credit or during the summer. Most of these internships are unpaid and while I realize there are ethical concerns with requiring unpaid work of people, the reality is that if you don't do internships while you are an undergraduate or graduate student, you will be doing them *after* you graduate because you're not likely to land a position without one or several of them. Does this favor people who can afford not to work one summer? Unfortunately, it does—but it's quite competitive to get positions in this field and they can afford to ask that you come with some experience, able to hit the ground running. There are ways around the unpaid conundrum too—do a virtual internship so you can also do a part-time job on the side, live with family members or friends during your internship to cut down on costs (I lived in the Cambridge, Massachusetts YWCA during one of my internships; I have several friends who waitressed during theirs), or work to save up some money to support yourself during an internship.

But internships are pretty much non-negotiable these days in almost any field, but especially in editing and publishing.

What if you're far from your undergrad days but you've decided to go in the direction of editing and publishing? Well, you can still pick up some of the courses you might need online from places like Mediabistro.com or you could spend the money on an iconic six-week publishing course through Columbia University, NYU, or the University of Denver. While expensive ($8,000 including food and lodging), most people who attend these intensive courses say they do give them an advantage in understanding, through lectures and hands-on experience, the latest developments in the publishing world and in building the necessary network to land an entry-level job. These courses can also be helpful for new graduates trying to get their foot in the door whose internship experience is limited. My caveat would be to do at least one internship before spending the money on this program, however, as a few of my students who have done internships in editing and publishing learned, more than anything, that they really didn't want to work in editing and publishing after all.

Libraries

Another field that many writers find rewarding to work in is library science. The benefits are, after all, obvious: You're surrounded by books and their readers, and, in much the same way that publishers and editors are (but perhaps at a different pace), you are also witness to the latest trends in writing and publishing. Famous librarian-writers include Proust, Beverly Cleary, Jessamyn West, Philip Larkin, and Anne Tyler. In fact, several of my former students now support their writing in this way. Some simply applied for librarian positions after undergraduate or graduate school with no further preparation—

these are not actually professional librarians but library staff nonetheless—while others pursued further degrees in library science to enable themselves to become professional librarians. Nonetheless, I keep up with several alumni librarians these days and most of them seem happy with their work and productive in their writing.

Bookstores

Another way to support yourself while writing is to work in a bookstore. While this may seem to be a run-of-the-mill minimum-wage job, there are a number of writers who have chosen this work (Jonathan Letham, David Mitchell, Emma Straub, and Meghan McCarthy, among others) who find it not only comforting to work among the written word but who also find it a real education in which books find readers and which ones don't and how the industry works.

Teaching

Teaching. Ah, teaching. I love it. The moment I started teaching in 1990, started talking words and language with other people, freeing them to write, to see themselves as writers, I knew I had found the career for me. Also, I am one of those people who found their groove in college and who can think of nothing better than to spend the rest of my days helping others find theirs in the same place. Higher education has changed a lot since I started in it, though. As universities hire fewer and fewer full-time, tenure-track professors, the jobs get harder and harder to find and that's saying something, since it wasn't easy when I went on the job market in 1997. I applied for hundreds of jobs. It's not impossible though—if you really love it, if teaching creative writing is what you want to do more than anything else in the world, you can probably make it happen. But you'll need an MFA *and a few published books*, or a Ph.D. and a strong publishing record. And a hell of a lot of persistence and perseverance. You have to really, really want to do it. Just like writing itself.

Then there's teaching high school. With the right background (a traditional or non-traditional teaching certificate), it's easier to get a job teaching high-school writing than college writing. Far easier, and the pay is about the same, maybe slightly higher for the high-school teacher. But from what I understand from the many high-school teachers I have worked with over the years, teaching high school these days is grueling work. It's not the kind of work that leaves much time or energy left over for your own writing. And you don't really have the summers off either—there's a lot of professional development you're required to do over during that time to maintain your teaching certificate. This isn't to say that you can't make a great difference in young people's lives as a high-school teacher and somehow manage to eke out some writing time. I've known a few people who managed to do it, but very, very few. Also, I caution against considering teaching high school as some kind of fallback position—teaching high school is only for the most passionate among us who want to pass on the love of language to those who need it most. Given the educational atmosphere today, anyone who goes into teaching who isn't passionate about it will be eaten alive. Over my twenty-five-year career, for example, I've taught a handful of students who had this passion, who I knew, as they sat in my creative writing classes proclaiming their desire to teach the next generation, would succeed. They are all amazing teachers today and if you had a child, believe me, you would want him or her sitting in their classrooms. The others, the ones who only considered teaching half-heartedly or as a fallback, are either already out of the profession after less than five years or trying to get out. Even though they are not paid or respected accordingly, it has long been my belief that only the best and the brightest among us survive and thrive as high-school teachers. Consider this advice carefully if it's the route you want to take.

Web content

Recently, many of my students have found great success writing content for websites. I don't necessarily mean freelance blogging—although I believe anyone graduating from college today should have a strong grasp of social media for business—but actual content creation and management for websites. Several write copy (similar to catalog copy) for the website of a major department store in the South, while others are full-time writers for lifestyle and financial websites. How did they get these positions? Again, they made sure to combine their creative writing courses with courses on information design and technical writing. Many of them also did internships at the very same places where they ended up working—again proving the importance of the intern experience.

Technical writing

As technology and the Web expand, so does the need to translate what happens there into clear, concise layperson's terms. There is a whole field that exists, technical writing, to teach you how to do this, and most universities offer a broad selection of courses in this field to prepare you. Technical writing pays fairly well, too. Some major cities even have professional staffing companies that provide temporary technical writing jobs for people who want to support themselves this way between creative projects—when I lived in the Washington, D.C. area I often supplemented my summer salaries with lucrative technical writing assignments with companies such as Sprint. It's definitely worth looking into.

Whenever he's asked about the viability of choosing a writing career, creative nonfiction writer and longtime teacher Dinty W. Moore usually replies, "none of my students are starving." This is the bold truth. None of the people I studied for an MFA with are starving either—far from it. They are all successful people with diverse careers and none of them strayed too far from their love of words. Several teach and have won teaching awards. Several are Web content creators—a few in fact, were in on Yahoo! at the beginning, and as you can imagine, are doing quite well—some are technical writers and editors. But they are all successful people who still write and enjoy a professional life steeped in the literary arts. And they are still writing. With some planning and foresight, the same kind of life is possible for you.

7

Being teachable

The one thing that matters more than talent

Over twenty-five years of living in the creative writing world have given me a unique perspective on the relative successes of my colleagues and students and the traits that led them to those successes. Talent is one trait, persistence another, passion and work ethic (or their synonyms) still others. But over the years, I've come to believe that perhaps the most important trait a new writer can possess is to be teachable. Do you want to further your education as a writer because you are curious, because you like to learn new things and don't believe you know it all yet, and because you are thrilled at the prospect of bringing all that you are learning to bear on your nascent writing abilities? That is what makes you teachable—and over time, it *will* make you a better writer.

Why are these qualities so important? Well, most of all, because in my experience, they result in more improvement over time, more "aha" moments when students realize how to take their writing to the next level. I have another, admittedly more selfish, reason: Students like this are a joy to teach, and while they certainly exist, in an increasingly test-driven society that rewards innate ability, they are not as common as you might think.

As anyone who has taken and taught dozens of creative writing workshops over the years knows, certain tropes emerge out of this particular classroom. One of them is the "Workshop Egotist," the student who doesn't feel he has anything to learn, and who is in the workshop only because he is seeking a teacher who will quickly reinforce his beliefs that, unlike his classmates, his writing has already "arrived." He disdains most of the readings, unless they confirm his current knowledge or beliefs, and likewise resists any information the teacher might be trying to impart that doesn't match up with the literary world as he has understood it up until that point (especially if it doesn't match up with the teachings of former mentors who have already confirmed his talent).

Workshop Egotists are also important for you to know about—because you need to learn how to deal with them in writing groups and in writing classrooms so that they don't overly influence your own work.

Wherever two or more gather to respond to one another's writing, the Workshop Egotist is likely to appear. Getting feedback for your writing is important; it's often a microcosm of your reading audience. But it needs to be the right kind of writing group, one that isn't dominated by these kinds of people, for writing groups dominated by Workshop Egotists can quickly become toxic. Avoid them if you can. To assist you, let me offer:

The field guide to the workshop egotist

1   In their many years of workshop experience (translation: one to three), Workshop Egotists have pledged their troths to the myth of the antagonistic, Bobby Knight-style of workshop experience, where no criticism is "sugar-coated" and everyone

"tells it like it is." (For the uninitiated, Bobby Knight is an abusive, chair-throwing college basketball coach.) It has never occurred to them that people like Bobby Knight might have had personality disorders that rendered them constitutionally unable or unwilling to translate hostile thoughts and words into constructive critique (something that eventually got Knight, and others like him, fired). Often, they will also show a barely concealed disdain for any workshop leader who is not similarly "tough enough" on their peers' work.

2   Likewise, Workshop Egotists believe that there are times when their teacher/leader should just tell a peer to give up on writing, that they are not one of the anointed and never will be. Workshop Egotists' confidence in this belief is usually directly related to the extent to which they exude the certainty that such advice would *never* be given to them.

3   When it is time for their work to go before the group, Workshop Egotists like to clear their throats and make pronouncements like, "Don't hold back, now. I'm tough. I can take it." Really. These are direct quotes and one of the easiest ways to recognize the Workshop Egotist in his or her natural habitat.

4   Workshop Egotists don't actually mean this. "I can take it," is instead code for one of the following: "I don't really believe anyone will actually find fault with my work"; "I am confident in my ability to rationalize away any considered suggestions the class or the leader has made"; or, my favorite, "I was just messing around with this piece anyway. It's not, like, serious work or anything I care about."

5   Workshop Egotists like to co-teach with the workshop leader whenever possible. Especially if the egotist is a male and the

workshop leader is a female (although the mark of a true Workshop Egotist is their desire to co-teach no matter the gender permutation). After all, they have so much wisdom to impart. Why hide their proverbial light under a bushel?

So why am I sharing this field guide with you? Well, because I wish someone had shared something like it with me thirty years ago. It probably would have spared me a lot of uncertainty as I tried to determine whose feedback to pay attention to and whose to ignore in my development as a writer, to figure out who genuinely cared about my work, and who was just posturing and angling to turn the workshop into yet another contest. Who knows, it might even spare the young workshop leader who hasn't had the benefit of time to watch these all too human patterns emerge again and again.

Workshop Egotists are difficult to mentor, resistant as they are to your attempts to impart what they don't already know. But what is most frustrating of all is decades of experience that tells me that these kinds of students don't usually succeed, because ultimately, they don't grow as writers. Eventually, whatever talent they started out with pales in comparison to that of their peers who are open to learning, and whose work is developing by leaps and bounds. Ultimately, they stop persisting because their work ethic is dependent on their work being praised and their genius acknowledged—a rare occurrence outside the classroom.

A recent article by Maria Popova in Brainpickings.org, "Fixed vs. Growth—The Two Basic Mindsets that Shape Our Lives,"[1] bears out these observations. According to the article, "a 'fixed mindset' assumes that our character, intelligence and creative ability are static givens which we can't change in any meaningful way ... and success is the affirmation of that inherent intelligence." On the other hand, "a 'growth mindset' thrives on challenge and sees failure not as evidence of a lack of intelligence, but as a springboard for growth." Not surprisingly, "the consequences of believing intelligence and personality can be developed . . . are remarkable."

Think about it: If you believe this, you *will* be open to learning more as a writer or as an artist. And if you don't believe it, if you think your talents are innate or "carved in stone," you will act out of an "urgency to prove yourself again and again."

Popova's article is in part a summary of Stanford Psychologist Carol S. Dweck's book, *Mindset: The New Psychology of Success*, in which she reports countless studies that support the triumph of the growth model. In fact, Dweck even studied subjects' brain waves as they "answered difficult questions and received feedback," and found that those with a fixed mindset were "only interested in hearing feedback that reflected directly on their present ability . . . tuning out information that could help them learn and improve," and even going so far as ignoring "the right answer when they had gotten a question wrong."[2]

What does this mean for aspiring writers and the writing classroom? As a writer, it's better to be teachable, to cultivate in yourself, as the article explains, a "passion for learning, rather than a hunger for approval." I'm reminded of a student who once cornered me after a community writing workshop in which everyone had spent a great deal of time discussing his story, commending what worked and making thoughtful suggestions for improvement. "They obviously don't like it," he said conspiratorially, in a last-ditch effort to get me to agree with him that "they" were wrong. Unfortunately, "they" had given this writer's story a great compliment: They had read it carefully, and they had given a lot of consideration to how he might make it better. Because this writer was acting out of a "fixed mindset," however, he refused to listen to anything but praise for his work. Sadly, this mindset will never get him anywhere.

How should you use this information in your writing career? First of all, maintain your curiosity about the world, especially the literary world, which evolves and changes as a natural course. Does this mean you should accept every new trend that emerges? Of course not. But try to consider new ideas and information with an open mind before rejecting anything out of hand. Think about why you might accept or not accept a new idea. Is there anything in your prior learning experience that might be affecting your perspective? Are you clinging to a past belief because that's what you've been told or what you've always done before? What's the worst that would happen if you tried something new—considered a new book you wouldn't normally read, a new writing practice, or technique?

Second, do some soul-searching when you receive feedback—from a teacher or a colleague. When you ask for feedback, be honest with yourself. What do you really want to hear? Do you really want to know where to go next with this piece? Or do you only want suggestions that confirm your abilities as a writer? Understand that literary art—*any* art—is 95 percent failure. That means that failure is good, that failure means you are taking risks and trying new things that may not necessarily work or make you look good—or be the kind of writing that has always "worked for you in the past." Reevaluate how you really feel about failure and whether you have a craving for success and recognition that might be an obstacle to your growth as a writer.

Third, really think about why you are writing and what might happen if you don't meet with the teacher or reader approval you seek. Will you be able to continue writing? Are you able to take long periods of rejection in stride and keep showing up at your desk the next day to continue the work of failing, and failing and failing until you finally find your voice? This is the reality of writing. You must be able to tolerate a lot of uncertainty, long periods of doing the work without knowing if anyone cares or is listening.

I've been working on my most recent novel for over two years now. I've shared two drafts with my agent six months apart and while her suggestions, as always, have been spot on, she doesn't think either of them are realizing the potential of this book. This amounts to months of work agonizing over two separate 65,000-plus word drafts that I felt pretty good about, that I felt were the best work I had done so far, only to be told, "not yet, back to the drawing board." How should I respond to this news? Well, I could respond by trying to get another agent— this book has been long-listed for two awards so far. Maybe my agent is wrong.

But maybe she's right. After all, she's always been an incredibly perceptive reader in the past, and that's what I like about her. As hard as it is to face that drawing board, to realize that two years into this project and not getting any younger, if I want this book to be the best book it can be, I may have to radically re-think my original ideas about it. I have to be willing to take some parts "down to the studs" and rebuild. This requires no small amount of soul-searching—and a lot of openness to what can be done differently, to the true meaning of the word revise, to totally reVISIONing the work.

And it means being comfortable with trying again—and maybe failing again, even, as long as I'm committed to this book—until I get it right. Not just reworking a paragraph here and there but reconsidering hours and hours of work, with nary a "gold star" in sight.

What if I never get it right?

Fortunately, I'm beyond gold stars, or I like to think I am—most of the time. I'm willing to go back to the material and just "be" with it, work with it, whether or not I ever achieve anything with it—until it finally works on the level it needs to or it teaches me the lesson it needs to teach. This is a hard reality to face and it's one that turns back many a writer who lives for praise and success. But it's a lesson most writers have faced at one time or another, often more than once. Ask any of them. Being teachable, open, even to teaching yourself, will help you overcome this kind of long-term uncertainty.

Lacking this growth mindset, however, has been the downfall of many a writer, in fact of many friends and students over the years who were unable to overcome their dependence on praise and who met the lack of it by growing bitter and resentful and withdrawing from their own work. Most of them are no longer writing. And that is the gravest failure at all.

Notes

1   Popova, Maria. "Fixed vs. Growth: The Two Basic Mindsets that Shape Our Lives," Brainpickings.org, accessed January 31, https://www.brainpickings. org/2014/01/29/carol-dweck-mindset/.

2   Ibid.

8

Writing 2.0 or, platform-building can be fun

It is for me anyway. That's because my "platform" is an organic part of me, the way I live in the world as a writer. But before I go on, you're probably wondering: What the heck is a platform and do I even need one? Let me explain.

Once upon a time, all you needed to do to be a writer was to write and publish your writing. That's still true if you are happy to focus solely on your writing and are less concerned with publishing it. But if you plan to publish, platform is important. In a world where we are constantly bombarded with text demanding our attention, *your* writing, *your* text, demands a platform to help it get noticed. The good news is that if you're mindful about it, you can build an organic platform that represents just another dimension of who you are as a writer, becoming part of your work rather than siphoning energy from it. Platform is your visibility as a writer, especially to your target audience. It's a mash-up of your personal and professional connections and your social media. It's why, more and more, when submitting a book to an independent press, whether poetry, fiction, or creative nonfiction, you'll be asked, "How will you help sell this book?"

Do you need a platform right now? If you're just starting out as a writer, no, you don't. You need to be putting most of your energies into writing and all the ways we've discussed so far that you can develop as a writer—classes, writing groups, workshops, and so forth. But while you're doing that, you also need to be sending out preliminary signals to your literary community, as discussed in Chapter 4. That's how platform-building starts, that's how you begin to make professional and personal connections, by becoming involved in and promoting literary culture in person and on social media—something you're already interested in. Right?

Unfortunately, platform-building is dogged by two persistent myths. The first is that it's all about self-promotion. The second is that it's only about the "marketplace." For example, a lot of students (and a lot of authors who clutter up my Twitter feed with tweets about their own publications and nothing else) think that literary citizenship and platform-building means nothing more than promoting their own work.

In reality, platform-building is about completely saturating yourself in literary culture—and then curating and promoting the work that interests you, so that other people will find it and care about it as much as you do. My own platform has been built on promoting other writers in whose work I'm deeply interested and in sharing information about writing and publishing. When I read a book I love or find an essay or poem that speaks to me, I want to tell the world about it. And it's not quid pro quo. I'm participating in—and perpetuating—this culture *because I love it*. Certainly, platform-building has commercial benefits for books and publishing, but what's at stake is much, much greater than that.

Beyond supporting literary culture, platform-building is also about becoming deeply involved in those subjects that interest you, even those that transcend writing itself, and sharing them with your community. This is more true if you're a creative nonfiction writer who writes about a particular subject and less so if you are a fiction writer (although fiction and poetry publishers will still want to know how you plan to help sell your book and your platform will come in handy then). For example, Heather Sellers, author of *You Don't Look Like Anyone I Know*, a memoir about her own face-blindness and family mental illness, writes a great deal about these subjects on social media. She's written articles for *O Magazine* and, importantly, for *Psychology Today*, confirming that, in fact, she's an expert on the subject of experiencing these illnesses in herself and others. Although she has also written many wonderful books in several genres (including some great ones about writing that are listed in the Appendix), her writing on face-blindness and family dysfunction remains a large part of her platform, something she built long before *You Don't Look Like Anyone I Know* was even published. Writers Anna Leahy and Doug Dechow, who have a passion for science, flight, and space exploration, wrote a popular blog, Lofty Ambitions, for years, before their book, *Generation Space: A Love Story* was published.

Fiction writer Cathy Day has written a great deal about teaching creative writing, especially the novel, and she also shares what's going on with her novel about Mrs Cole Porter, revealing historical tidbits about the famous composer's wife here and there as she discusses the progress of her novel. This is a way of building interest in it in advance. And while writing about writing is also one of my "subjects" (hence the book you're holding in your hands), I often share the process of working on my other novels, which also take place at certain points in history. When I visited the graves of the victims of the General Slocum Disaster, the greatest disaster to hit New York City before 9/11, I posted photos on my various social media sites and shared information about this little-known tragedy that begins my current novel.

So some of platform-building is what writer and platform specialist Austin Kleon would call "showing your work," maximizing the aspect of art that is communal—the desire among artists, in this case writers, to know what one another are working on and how the process works for them. Showing your work—and being interested when others show theirs—is part of being intensely curious about how art and the world works. That's what good artists do.

Should you start by sharing wildly about everything you're working on? Not unless you feel deeply compelled to. In the beginning, make the connections and simply follow the outlets that feel most comfortable to you. In this way, social media will become more important to you professionally than personally. Perhaps you used to follow certain social media accounts, those of celebrities and so forth, just for "fun." But you can also learn a lot about following people who are also immersed in fields to which you aspire. My son, for example, who wants to be a concert cellist, focuses on practicing several hours a day. But he also keeps up with teachers and students at all of the best conservatories on social media—not only because he is naturally interested in what they're doing but also because they are a few steps ahead of him and following them teaches him a great deal about the classical music world. You can do the same thing in writing.

Likewise, although I had written for years, my own foray into platform-building began without me even realizing it. I started reading blogs around ten years ago, which was also around the same time I joined Twitter and Facebook. I read blogs about creative writing and some other more personal topics (home design, crafts, family life) for well over a year, "lurking," some might say, before I started to feel I might have something to add and started a blog of my own. Even then, after that, I blogged for five more years, developing my own blogging voice and style and narrowing in on my subject (writing about writing and teaching creative writing) before I got my break at the *Huffington Post*. By then, my voice had matured and I was ready for a larger outlet.

How do you decide which social media outlets to pursue? It really comes down to whatever feels most natural to you. In the past several years, I've tried several "social media" apps with varying success—Instagram, Tumblr, Pinterest, Goodreads, Twitter—but I always come back to Facebook, for whatever reason, perhaps my Generation X roots. While I post on Twitter from time to time when I want to share information and I do enjoy reading the accounts of writers and editors there, Facebook is the site that always pulls me in. So it makes the most sense that while I might maintain presences on several platforms, Facebook is the one I will concentrate on because it comes the most naturally to me and is where I'm most likely to draw the largest readership, with Twitter coming in a close second. I don't have a huge number of followers—but the people who do follow me on that site often come up to me and tell me that they appreciate the information I post there and tell people who are starting out as writers to follow me too.

That doesn't mean I'm not open to whatever comes along in the future. As writers, we simply have to be open to changes in the publishing and literary world, and that means changes in technology and in the social media world that it participates in (and where, in the absence of bookstores and book reviews, ever more readers find their books). Who knows what fabulous platform is waiting to materialize to promote writing and reading just around the corner? Whatever it is, we need to be ready to take advantage of it in whatever way that feels most natural to us.

9

Traditional book publishing today: Finding and working with an agent

Writing a book is challenging work that takes more perseverance and dedication to one task than most people find appealing. But we've already established that you're not most people: You're a writer, you write. And if you write prose long enough, it's entirely possible that you may be seduced enough by the idea of writing a book into actually writing one. After all, if you're already making the effort into putting what you have to say, what you need to say, on paper, it won't be long before the pages start to accumulate.

There are some good resources out there about actually crafting book-length work listed in the Appendix, from the National Novel Writing Month website to Donald Maas' famous *Writing the Breakout Novel*—I cannot recommend them enough as guides to getting you through the woods of a big project. These next three chapters will pick up once you've finished, however—an achievement that should first be celebrated all by itself (seriously, break out the champagne or whatever you prefer, and hoist a glass)—and are ready to seek publication, first by finding and developing a relationship with an agent and later, going on submission in the hopes of breaking into one of the "big five" or an independent publisher, or, if you want to cut to the chase, self-publishing your work.

Why should I find an agent?

If you've written a book of prose for the adult market—fiction or creative nonfiction—and you have any hopes of reaching a wide audience through a big five or major independent publisher, you must have an agent. You can't submit to these publishers any other way. This is a little different in the children's lit market—agents are still important but there are other ways, especially through editor's appearances at regional and national children's conferences, to get through to the major publishers. But in adult publishing, agents are required. They are the people with the industry contacts and experience who can get your work read by editors at the major presses and who know which editors are looking for what kind of work. As if that weren't enough, they are often terrific editors as well (mine is) who can help you take your manuscript to the next level. And they are critical for negotiating your contracts with publishers and making sure your best interests are represented. Finally, the best agent does not represent one book but you as an author, and your whole career.

So how do I get one?

There are passive and active ways to find an agent. Seeking an agent passively is kind of like seeking passive income; it's something that you do by being smart about how you represent yourself. For example, you eventually aim to publish your work in venues with broad audiences where an agent might discover you and ask to see more of your work. I have been approached by agents for my work in the *Huffington Post* column that led to this book, for example. I have also been approached by agents when one of my novels was long-listed in a major competition. For this reason, whenever you publish something with a bio or whenever your biography appears in writing, you should always mention that you are working on a book because that, along with the quality of your writing, will grab an agent's attention. You could also participate in one of the many agent pitch contests on Twitter and other social media. You could use one of the many reference books on agents published each year—although these are expensive, as they go out of date quickly. Or you could just go about your agent search the new-old-fashioned way, by researching agents online through websites such as AgentQuery.com or QueryTracker. com, making a long list of possible agents for your book, researching each agent or agency again via their own website, and in the process, annotating and prioritizing your list by order of agents you:

1   feel would be most likely to get your book published;
2   feel would work with you most closely on your vision for your book and your career.

This is what I recommend because this is what worked for me.

What you need to do

Finding an agent the new-old-fashioned way can take significant time and effort, although discovering someone who can champion your work in the publishing industry is well worth it. Before you begin, you need to assemble a few items for the journey. The first of these is a finished draft of your book that is as close to perfect as you can possibly get it—it's been critiqued by mentors, beta readers, or writing group members, and you've revised and edited and revised and edited until you can barely see straight. It needs to be this "finished," because some agents are going to request full manuscripts or the first few chapters right away (if you're submitting fiction or narrative nonfiction; some other forms of nonfiction work can be submitted on the basis of a few sample chapters and a proposal) and you want to be able to send them the best work you can. You also need a query letter and a one-page synopsis. The Appendix here will feature some good Web resources on writing query letters and synopses but the idea to remember about these is that the query letter for an agent is like the cover letter for a journal—it's what shows an agent you're a serious writer and gets them interested in your book. The synopsis is a one-page, single-spaced summary of the whole work, including spoilers, to show them how the work unfolds and help them decide if they want to request a full draft. Agents receive hundreds of queries a week—if they requested full drafts from everyone who queried them, they'd be mainlining vitamin D because they'd never leave their desks. Based on your stellar query, you want to make sure yours is the draft they request.

Once you're all packed and ready to go, you can start researching agents at the following sites. In fact, writing the query letter and the synopses has already prepared you really well for getting down to the nitty-gritty of what kind of book you've written in terms of genre and subgenre, theme, topic, and so forth. This will make the agent search easier. Both AgentQuery.com and QueryTracker.com offer useful ways to search for agents using different keywords and searches that include agents with particular genre interests as well as agents that are looking for new work. QueryTracker.com has the added benefit of offering a tracker that you can use to monitor the responses that you get to your queries, but if you choose to use it, you have to agree to let the site use information from it in the aggregate, so they can gather information on response times and practices from different agents. Both sites offer the kinds of information in their agent entries that will help you decide if an agent is worth researching further and approaching, and can even help you rank your list, if you're so inclined. This information includes how long the agent has worked in the industry and where, what subjects and genres they're particularly interested in, and what authors and books they have represented in the past.

This is where the process becomes time-consuming—and you've only just begun—in terms of research and information management. You're going to want a pretty long, detailed, well-researched list of agents to begin with—if you like to create Excel files, this is your lucky day!—because the more you learn about an agent, the more you can talk to them in your query letter about why you want *them*, in particular, to represent your work. Because ultimately, you really want to make a good match with your agent, someone who really gets what you're doing and wants to champion it—and discerning which agent that might be is a time-intensive endeavor.

Once you've settled on your list, you will want to take your time going through it, a process that could take weeks or months (unless this is the only thing you have to do all day, in which case, you might complete all of this work in a week or two). You'll want to research these agents not only by reading about what they are looking for and how your work should be submitted to them but by reading interviews they've done and articles they've written online. You might also start following several of them on Twitter—a great way to find out what kind of person they might be, what they're looking for, and to find out more about what an agent's life is like in today's publishing world (like most people in the industry, they are working their butts off).

Because doing this is so time-consuming and tiring, I recommend submitting via email (how it's done these days) to no more than five agents a day. Otherwise, all that information starts to blur together and the chance that you might address an agent by another's name or commit some other faux pas starts to rise. You really don't want to do that. It won't end your career or anything, but it will dent your chances with that particular agent.

As you're doing your research, also be certain that you're dealing with a legitimate agent. Besides having a strong industry track record, legitimate US agents will belong to the Association of Authors Representatives, the literary agent trade association. Likewise, credible UK agents will belong to the Association of Authors' Agents. Legitimate agents won't ask you for any money upfront to read your manuscripts or work with you. Agents receive an industry-standard 15 percent commission once they sell your work, but they should not request anything from you before that. Nor should they suggest that your book needs serious editing or "book doctoring," as it's called, and they have a "friend" they can refer you to for that service—for a fee. This is a common scam. An agent will either work with you to get your book ready for submission as part of their services, or they may suggest you need an editor—but they won't "happen" to have one in mind at the ready. At least scrupulous ones won't.

If you have any concerns about an agent, editor, or publisher, it's always a good idea to do some research on them. Start with a Google search but also look them up on Preditors and Editors, an aptly named site that actually lists nefarious publishing industry concerns to avoid, and read what's been said about them on the Absolute Write forums or other writers' forums.

Once you send a query to an agent (almost always via email; they will have specific instructions on their website and each agent's instructions are a little different), they can respond in a few ways. If intrigued, they will request you send either a full or partial manuscript, which they will respond to in time, after you send it. If not, they will either respond with a polite rejection after an appropriate period of time, or, if they have noted as such on their website, they may be so overrun with queries that if you do not hear from them after a certain period of time, you can assume the answer is no.

The common wisdom is that for every ten queries, a quality manuscript will get a full or partial request and that it takes ten full or partial requests to finally land an agent. Do the math—that's up to 100 query letters you will have to send out. Yes, up to 100 query letters sent to agents you have researched well as being favorably inclined toward your book out of the 1,000 or so agents working in America today. If you're lucky, you'll find your agent before that, but be prepared to put in the time. Create a preliminary list of about 100 agents, tiered, you would like to submit to, and then begin researching and submitting to about five agents per day or at a sitting.

When you get "the call"

I landed my agent, Anne Bohner at the Pen and Ink Literary Agency, after about twenty-six submissions and three requests for partials of my first novel, *The Lost Son*. I had a feeling, after reading the website for her boutique agency (she's a one-woman show), learning about the books and the authors she represented, and reading interviews with her that I found online, that she understood the stories I was trying to tell in my novels and I tried to make this connection in my query letter with her. I was excited but not completely shocked when she seemed interested and ultimately asked if we might discuss the novel over the phone.

This, my friends, is what's known among authors as, "the call." Agents don't use that term, because they might phone you about other issues before taking you on. But we authors love to fuss about "the call." When an agent asks, "I'd like to talk to you about your work, when can we discuss this over the phone?," it's almost always good news. It's also a phone call you should be prepared for. If you've got a particularly good manuscript on your hands, you might even have more than one agent who wants to represent you, so you have several "calls" during which you might suss out how different agents might represent you and promote your career as a whole. As a general rule, come with a list of questions. Again, make sure you know as much as you can about your agent—some of the answers to basic questions (such as who they have represented in the past) can be learned beforehand. Otherwise, as a general rule, be pleasant, be positive, be ready to talk about your work—the project at hand as well as future projects you are planning (and you better be planning some; your agent probably doesn't want to represent just one work)—and feel free to ask what the next steps will be. When will you sign a contract? When does the agent plan to submit your work and what kind of revision will happen before then? My agent, who I have nicknamed "the manuscript whisperer," used to be an editor for Penguin and she really helped me take *The Lost Son* to the next level; she seems to know how to put her finger on just the right revisions. How will the submission process work and how will your agent contact you during this time?

Once you've had the call and have an agent, it's time again to stop and celebrate. As you have just read, it's not easy to land an agent, just as it's not easy to finish a book. That said, it's important to celebrate each success along the way to ready yourself for the next one, which in this case, is going "on submission," a whole new level indeed. So raise a glass, tell all your friends, have a celebratory dinner—do whatever you can to mark the fact that you have just made it a little further along the author's journey. And get ready for the next step.

10

Making the show: They said "No." Now what? Or, they said "Yes!" Now what?

In the classic 1980s romantic comedy, *Bull Durham*, about minor league baseball in North Carolina, longtime minor league player, "Crash" Davis (Kevin Costner) waxes rhapsodic to his younger teammates on the team bus about what it's like to make "the show," that is, what it's like to be called up to the big leagues to play:

> Yeah, I was in the show. I was in the show for twenty-one days once—the twenty-one greatest days of my life. You know, you never handle your luggage in the show, somebody else carries your bags. It was great. You hit white balls for batting practice, the ballparks are like cathedrals, the hotels all have room service...'[1]

Publishing your book with one of the big five publishers—HarperCollins, Penguin Random House, Simon & Schuster, Macmillan, and Hachette and their dozens of imprints—or with a major independent publisher such as Bloomsbury, Algonquin, Melville House, or Two Dollar Radio, is the dream of many an author, just as the big leagues are where minor league ball players hope to spend their careers. Publishing with these houses is also the goal of your agent and why you have one. These are the publishers that pay substantial advances, and without a real advance, your agent doesn't make any money. They are also the publishers who have the resources and the mechanisms to support an author at every step of the process, from acquisition through the various stages of editing, launch, and book promotion. This doesn't mean that as an author you're not required to do a great deal of heavy-lifting along the way, especially in terms of responding to edits and promoting your work. But the major publishers have been selling books for a long time and they know what they're doing.

They're also extremely difficult to break into, even with an agent. Some reports say that about 50 percent of agented manuscripts sell, while other industry insiders say even those numbers are too hard to pin down and estimates might be even lower.

Once you've signed with an agent, they'll want to do everything in their power to increase those odds. First and foremost, this means that they'll want to submit what they see as a perfect manuscript. So, you know how you revised your manuscript until your eyes bled? That's great!! You probably learned a lot from that revision and it helped you get the representation you have now. But you ain't seen nothing yet— because your shrewd agent probably has several more revisions in store for you before your manuscript is submission-ready.

This prediction is not only based on my own experience (remember, my agent is "the manuscript whisperer") but on the stories of countless others in the industry. As the pressure rises on editors to acquire best-sellers right out of the gate, the agent–author relationship has become in many ways the kind of editing relationship that was once more common between editors and authors, such as the oft-recalled relationship between Maxwell Perkins and F. Scott Fitzgerald many decades ago. The current state of affairs is not surprising when you consider that a lot of agents, mine included, used to be editors, and often went into agenting later so that they could work more with authors one-on-one. This doesn't mean editors will completely let you off the hook in terms of revision, just that they want you to be pretty far along by the time the manuscript gets to them.

At this point, all the years you've put in dedicated to your writing should pay off because you know that all good writing is really re-writing and you're probably eager to put into practice all the shrewd insights your agent has given you into taking your manuscript up another notch. You're taking her editorial letters seriously and choosing your battles exceedingly carefully, avoiding rookie stuff like, "but that's how it happens in real life" (because we all know that real life and fiction are not the same thing by definition of the word, "fiction"). I took pretty much all the advice my agent gave me on my first book except in regards to the survival of one main character—I fell on my sword on that, even though I worked out ways to at least prolong this character's life. I just couldn't "see" this character surviving, it wasn't part of my vision for the book. In hindsight, with the book still unsold, I still wonder if perhaps I shouldn't have tried harder to come up with a better compromise. But overall, you get the picture: I chose my battles—I was inclined to agree with my agent most of the time and I know I have a better book because of it. I encourage you to be open to the same kinds of suggestions.

After you've spent a good several months (at least) in back and forth revision, your agent will finally decide you are ready to go on submission. You'll probably know you're reaching this point—she'll tell you as you're getting closer and eventually, she'll share with you her plans for submission, that is, who she plans to send your manuscript to and how she plans to tell you about the responses she gets. Most agents are fairly transparent this way and you should expect it—you need to know the kind of reaction your work is getting out in the world. My agent shared with me the "A" list—the first list of publishers, editors, and imprints she planned to submit to and when and then, as the reactions began to come in, she shared the email responses with me.

You'll be tempted, at first, to check your email constantly, which is, of course, totally normal. But you don't want to watch it so closely that you ignore the other parts of your writerly life, indeed, the most important part, because the first thing you should start doing, intensely, while you're on submission, is working on your next project! You want to do this for three main reasons. One, because it will remind you of the reason that you are doing this, that you are a writer, someone who tells stories, not someone who constantly stares bug-eyed at their inbox waiting for the numbers to change. Two, because being on submission can be a bit volatile emotionally—positive news one day (the editor at Conglomerate Press is taking the book to the sales committee!) and negative the next (the sales committee thought it was too much like something that has recently been published) in ways that some writers might find a bit paralyzing—but less so if they're already in the middle of something else. And finally, three, if you *do* sell your book, and the publisher is excited about it, they'll probably ask what else you're working on and if you have a proposal to sell them describing what that is—you may come out of being on submission with a sweet, two-book deal.

Another thing about being on submission: Remember how in grad school or in your writing group, people doled out harsh criticism with the excuse that they were just trying to toughen you up for the caustic rejections of the big bad editor? Turns out that's just a myth, because by the time your agented work is making the rounds, the editors seem to go to great pains to be kind. In fact, they can be so complimentary of the book, spouting lines like, "the writing was just wonderful and this is obviously a writer to watch," that you'll be wondering why they're rejecting it until you get to the inevitable version of, "I just didn't *love* it." Because that's what it comes down to. A publishing house will put tens of thousands of dollars into your book; an editor is putting her career on the line—they're going to have to love it if they do that. But until then, they're going to be really nice about saying, "No thanks." I'm told this is more about respect for the agent than anything else. After a while, though, it starts to feel like the publishing industry is populated by people who have modeled themselves after Chip-n-Dale. As my agent says, and I'm sure she's not alone, it just takes that one editor to love your work, to champion it. Will you find that person on submission? That's the mystery.

They said "Yes!" Now what?

So. You're on submission and you've cleared the first hurdle—the editor at Conglomerate Press is excited about your manuscript! That means he's going to make an offer, right? Not so fast: Depending on the house, you have to beat some other levels first—as if the submission process wasn't agonizing enough. At most houses, the editor will probably share your book with at least one other editor to see what they think. This is another gate where, of course, a project could get stopped in its tracks and alas, my own book has tripped at the "let me show this to my colleague" stage. But let's say you make it past this gate and the colleague likes your book too. Then they'll make an offer, right? Not yet! The next test is the next editorial meeting—your work is sent out to all the key editors in the house as well as the sales team, and at the next editorial meeting, your editor makes a presentation about why your book is *the* book they should be acquiring. Other books will be presented at this meeting, so this is a good time for all the editors to find out what books are being acquired and make sure there aren't any duplicates in terms of content or subject matter. At this point, *everyone* will discuss whether to acquire your book, so yay, time for my personal favorite: The group decision! If you've ever been part of a group decision—and as a human being, I'm guessing you've been privy to many—you know that these up the variables considerably. There's group dynamics, how each of several editors is feeling that day, whether the book that was presented before yours was met with great applause or disdain—hate to say it, but even the best books (and having made it this far, yours surely is up there) flounder at the editorial meeting stage. At this point, the editorial group may give a resounding "No, thanks," or they may ask your editor to bring some revisions back to you and ask to see it again. Or, they may actually say, "Oh my gosh, yes! This is wonderful. We'd be crazy not to publish this book!"

Congratulations!! Time to celebrate! Again! If you haven't noticed, I'm big on celebration, but I believe it's important to take the time to stop and mark your accomplishments. Otherwise, you get caught up on the endless treadmill of craving the next achievement instead of appreciating how far you've come. So, take a moment. Tell your family. Tell all your friends. Shout it from the rooftops. This is a big deal—after all, as you've probably figured out by now, publishing a book at this level is harder than the proverbial camel passing through the eye of a needle. Then, after the champagne glasses are put away, here's what you can expect.

It will probably take about twelve to eighteen months for your book to hit the shelves. After your publisher makes the offer, there's a contracting period during which they hash out terms with your agent, and this can take a few months. After the ink on the contracts is dry, you'll enter a period during which you may be asked to do some minor revisions for the editor—probably nothing too major, because that happened with your agent. Once these are complete, your manuscript will be sent to Production as the copy-editing process begins. Meanwhile, a lot has been going on behind the scenes as the publishing staff has met to determine the vision for the book, including the design and cover, and the promotions plan for before and after the first copy hits the shelves. You'll have some work to do during the production phase as well, in the final months leading up to publication. You'll receive proofs from the production editor and a request for you to mark any final corrections. At this point, these should be very minor—misspellings or typos, consistency, fact-checking. Anything more than that, anything that would require a major shifting of text, is pretty much verboten at this point.

If an advance is involved, you should get a check soon after you sign your contract. However, advances are rarely distributed all at once any more but rather at milestone points in the publication process—for example, half upon contract signing and half upon manuscript delivery. Finally, the check will not go to you directly but to your agent, who will deduct the 15 percent she has worked hard for and then cut you a check for the rest.

And then you wait. Hopefully, you've been working with the publisher to promote the book for months already, so you're not exactly sitting on your hands at this point. You're doing everything you can to help your publisher build buzz. So you're probably pretty busy, and nervous, and excited. And you should be! Because you have a book coming out. Enjoy the fanfare—and most important, keep working on the next one!

They said "No." Now what?

My agent had an "A" list and a "B" list which seemed to be related to how closely matched the manuscript was to the publisher and her connections, as well as to the publisher's clout. After we went through the "A" list without an offer, she went back through the manuscript with a general sense of the first set of editorial responses and set me to work on some revisions before approaching the "B" list. It was at this point, for example, when I decided to keep that one main character alive longer than he had been in the first version. I had a near acceptance that got my hopes up in this round—close enough that my agent told me to get the second book proposal ready, but ultimately the novel went unsold. So what did I do?

I grieved, yes—it's important to allow yourself to do that. But fortunately, my writing didn't really suffer because I was already well along on my next book. My agent suggested self-publishing my first novel if I really wanted to see the book in print—but I didn't want to go that route, mostly because I simply don't have the necessary time to devote to promoting it. She also freed me to submit the novel to other, less well-known independent publishers, those who don't offer advances, and this is something I have pursued in earnest.

I haven't given up on the book entirely—it was recently one of four finalists in an e-book competition, and I'm still looking for places it might land. It would mean a lot to me to see it in print: I still believe in the book; it did after all, get me the agent. But even if I do give up on it, eventually, that would be all right too. I've moved on and that book taught me a lot—there's no way I could have written my current novel without it. While on the one hand, each novel is its own territory whose map you must learn to navigate, that doesn't mean that the very act of writing a novel doesn't lead you in any number of ways, some impalpable, to the next one. And even if it didn't, even if that was the only novel I ever wrote, the journey of writing it, of weaving that story and creating those characters, of vexation, frustration, and joy, was magical. For people like us, the journey of writing always is. Is it extra work, sure, but not everyone gets to do it, not everyone feels so inspired, and given the choice of a life with or without a little magic, I would always choose a little magic.

Small consolations

When I first started to read about what it was like going on submission, I came upon several stories from writers who didn't sell their first novels, or even their second. There were a lot of them out there and that was some small consolation. But even if there hadn't been any, I already knew I was in good company. The publishing world is an awfully arbitrary place.

There was my husband, who in 2011 almost secured the agent of his dreams, the kind of agent who has represented many famous authors, authors you have definitely heard of, literary legends. The only problem with this kind of agent is that they are usually legends themselves, which means they are somewhat advanced in years. We will get back to that in a moment.

So my husband had written a very fine novel about Van Gogh's passions and compulsions and his years in Arles, and it had attracted the interest of this legendary agent which was a fortunate thing because as I mentioned before, my husband does absolutely nothing half-assed. He had poured years of his life and research into this book and it was actually several hundred pages long.

Legendary agent asked him to make a round of revisions, which my husband dutifully did. Legendary agent was pleased with these revisions. He turned the book over to his associate to get it into the pipeline. She read the book and liked it and also sent a list of revisions, which my husband completed, quickly returning the manuscript. And then he waited.

And waited. And waited.

Many months passed.

After an appropriate amount of time, my husband should have emailed legendary agent's associate to ask what was going on, correct? Sounds easy, right?

Of course. But legendary agent's associate had stopped answering her email. So had legendary agent.

Crickets.

Crickets. Crickets. Crickets.

Finally, after over a year and after my disappointed husband had given up on ever hearing from them again, he finally received an email from legendary agent. The reason for the radio silence—can you guess?

Legendary agent and legendary agent's associate were both pretty far on in years. Legendary agent's associate had died suddenly and apparently, she had been critical to keeping the agency running. Legendary agent was now completely overwhelmed and unable to figure out how to carry on the business. He was retiring now and closing the agency. He was, of course, terribly sorry.

And that, my friends, is the risk of being chosen by a legendary agent.

Has my husband bounced back? Of course. He never stopped writing—saddened as he was, nothing stops him from writing; the words literally gush from his pen. He went on to publish his next book, a collection of short stories (notoriously hard to place, but he did) with an outstanding literary publisher, Lavender Ink. The collection came out to great acclaim (our state newspaper's art critic compared him to Faulkner), and yet another publisher, Burlesque Press, is about to bring out his novel about the last days of Oscar Wilde. And he's already moved on to other projects.

To say the writer's life is a roller coaster, then, in terms of publication, is a bit of an understatement. Another story I like to tell, of hope and sorrow and hope again, is of my former student, Brandi Lynch, a first-year student in the spring of 2000 and as fresh-faced and dewy-eyed about writing, about college, about everything, as she could possibly be. Bright, eager, sitting up so straight, when you looked over at her, Brandi was always grinning, brown eyes shining, long brown hair flowing down her back, obviously happy to be exactly where she was. Eventually, you start looking over at students like that a lot, because they make you feel like you might actually know what you're doing. She was also in the very first creative writing class I ever taught at my university, so I definitely needed some reassurance that I knew what I was doing.

First classes of anything are often memorable and so several students from that class remain imprinted in my mind, forever eighteen, just as I am forever thirty-two. But then life happens. Years pass and I see Brandi less and less in the classroom and more on the university grounds, now in a blue campus maintenance uniform with her name embossed on the pocket, expertly planting tulips in the front plot of our new building. Events intervened that required Brandi to become a maintenance employee in order to finish her degree, which took significantly longer than anticipated, although finish she would, eventually.

"I'm still writing," she tells me, when we stop to talk. And this time, it is me who grins. This, is a good sign, I think to myself, as I walk into the building. She's still writing.

Fast forward another five years, to spring 2008. Brandi is back again in my classroom, in another new course on how to live a creative life, how to make your own success as an artist and as a writer. Grinning still, happy as always, it seems, to be there. Listening, absorbing, she misses nothing.

Taking a page from Carolyn See's *Making a Literary Life*, I require students to write brief fan notes to writers they admire, making moves toward connecting to the literary world around them by giving back, showing appreciation to their favorite writers. Brandi wastes no time in emailing publishing wunderkind Christopher Paolini and a brief email exchange flutters between them. I remember musing at the time, that the two of them were probably around the same age.

At the end of that class, in an effort to drive home the message that tenacity is as important as talent in this writing life, I hand out slips of paper laser-printed with NEVER GIVE UP and my email address to each student (I still hand these out but now the message is printed on business cards with a graphic of Abraham Lincoln). Brandi and I return to greeting each other over dirt and tulips. She graduates with a Creative Writing degree. I know she's writing because she finds me on Twitter and we talk about our passion in cyberspace, writer to writer, supporting each other in this difficult life we have chosen, as if we had a choice. She starts a blog. She promotes other writers and books she is passionate about. And then . . .

One of my colleagues' keys are stolen and our whole building has to be re-keyed. Now promoted to Administrative Assistant at the Physical Plant (no more uniform, no more dirt), Brandi sits, back still straight, still smiling, in our conference room, distributing our new keys.

"I sold my book," she says softly as I finish signing the paperwork for my key. And then she tells me how this came about, how she sold *Lead Me Back Home* to Spencer Hill Press. It turns out there's even more to this story, more tenacity, more perseverance.

This is actually the fourth book one of our undergraduate writing alums has sold and I'm always thrilled for them. Always. I don't think it will ever get old. But there's something special about it this time. When I was thirty-two and first taught Brandi, I suspected that someone who poured that much energy and dedication into her work would succeed in the long run. But I had to grow older along with her, watch her story unfold, before my suspicions were confirmed.

Giddy over our students' success, I suggest that we invite three of these students who still live in the state to come to our next student writing conference to talk about their paths to publication. As the date nears, however, Brandi has some bad news. Spencer Hill Press was bought out and her editor laid off. Her book will not be published.

Fast-forward to the last months during which I am finishing this book. I checked back in with Brandi to see how her career was going and how she had dealt with that disappointment. The most recent news? She has gotten the rights back on *Lead Me Back Home* but she is "sitting on it" for now, while she works on several other projects for her new agent, her first agent, Nicole Resciniti at the Seymour Agency.

So what is the lesson here, besides perseverance?

While publication is often an end result of writing, that is not what it's *about*. Because if it were, these bitter disappointments would have encouraged these writers to just stop writing. It didn't, though, because they don't know how to do anything else. They are writers, people who make things out of words, who are constantly making things out of words, compulsively even, while the publishing world, an entirely different world, continues around them. They dip their toes in from time to time, sometimes they take a whole swim, of course, they want to be read.

But they would write regardless.

Note

1 Shelton, Ron. *Bull Durham*, directed by Ron Shelton. Beverly Hills, CA: MGM, 1988.

11

Non-traditional book publishing: What you need to know

The only certainty about the current state of literary affairs since the dawn of digital publishing and Web 2.0, is that it is in constant flux, with all parties concerned casting about for the next sure thing that will transform the industry. Until the dust settles, and I'm not sure it ever really will, all we can do as writers is hang on for the ride, keep writing, and try to keep up with what's going on, looking for opportunities to insert ourselves into this swirling world whenever we can.

Self-publishing and publishing-on-demand

One of the major players in publishing's shifting sands is printing-on-demand (or POD), which describes sites such as Createspace or lulu. com where you can upload your book of poetry, your literary magazine, your novel, and people can instantly order it online, in hard copy or as an ebook and have it delivered directly to them. Poof—the middle people, the agents, editors, and publishers, disappear. Not only has publishing-on-demand changed the way some small-scale independent publishers work, it has completely revolutionized self-publishing. In fact, I know a number of people who have published their work this way and not only have they made some money at it but more importantly, their work has gotten into the hands of readers who really enjoyed it, and when you get right down to it, isn't that what this is all about?

Here's the thing, from my perspective, the mid-level people in publishing are some of the most vital. Publishing entails a lot of players: Acquisitions editors, copy-editors, publicists and sales reps, just to name a few. In a large publishing company, these are all different people; in a small one, they might boil down to one or two. I appreciate all of them but I have a special place in my heart for editors. Editing is an art; something that only certain people can do well and usually an art that those very people have been cultivating for many, many years. Editors take what authors have given them, see the potential in it, and then carefully, painstakingly, work with the manuscript and the author until this potential is realized. The developmental editors I have worked with always challenged me to take my writing to the next level, asking all the right questions, probing further and deeper in ways I couldn't see myself because I was too close to the work. Without editors, almost everything I have ever published would be a mere shadow of itself.

This is to say nothing of copy-editors, whose meticulous efforts ensure that when my work finally greets the public, it will contain virtually no grammatical errors, inconsistencies, typos, or erroneous information; and, what's more, the writing itself will be stylistically air-tight. In short, even though I have proofread my work endlessly, aiming for the cleanest possible copy of which I am capable (and I am an above-average proofreader), it's the copy-editor who makes sure I don't embarrass myself. Copy-editing is much, much harder to do than people realize; in fact, it's a highly cultivated skill that is extremely time-consuming. After revising and copy-editing my work ad infinitum, asking my husband to do the same, then revising once more (and remember, we're both writers for whom editing comes as second nature), I am always astounded at what the copy-editor catches. This is why when someone who is self-publishing balks at paying to have the work professionally edited, I always die a little inside. Professional editors are worth every penny and are probably underpaid to boot. Whenever I read something that has been self-published, it's easy to tell whether or not the author has hired a professional copy-editor. Usually, they haven't.

The other important work publishers do is publicity and promotion. Good publicity—heck, even so-so publicity—involves a huge amount of effort and unless you have the time (and the budget) to devote to it (and the most successful self-published authors were also tireless self-publicists who *did* put in that time), it still is the very rare self-published book that will sell well. Even Amanda Hocking, the wunderkind of self-publishing, who has sold hundreds of thousands of books, admits that part of the reason she went to the "dark side" of traditional publishing (besides the fortune they offered her) is that she just wanted to focus on the writing and not all the other stuff that has to happen to get books sold. Hocking also has high praise for the editing process at publishing houses. When her self-published books were acquired by traditional publishers, they were all edited and re-written before they were released and, she acknowledges, the books are far better for it. In fact, she says quite clearly in her advice to writers that if there is any place that self-publishers tend to short-change their readers, it's in the editing.

As I've mentioned before, agents function the same way. Often former editors with years of experience, they have a keen eye for good storytelling and they know exactly what a story needs to make it effective, to make it the kind of experience that will leave the reader coming back for more. Once you take editors and agents with this keen eye out of the equation, good storytelling suffers. So if you're going to undertake the self-publication of your book in order to tell a great story and perhaps even make some money and enhance your writer's profile, do your homework. Learn everything you can about book publicity—truthfully, you should probably do this even if you're going the traditional publishing route, since most publishers also expect writers to contribute to publicity. Develop a promotion plan months ahead of the launch of your book and follow it. Hire a good freelance editor to make sure that your work delivers on the singular promise to transport the reader, without petty distractions, that every book makes. For that matter, hire a *real* graphic designer to create your cover rather than relying on your neighbor's sketches (unless your neighbor is a graphic designer). In short, there is nothing wrong with self-publishing. Printing-on-demand is changing the face and future of self-publishing, storming the gates and sidestepping barriers at every turn. But just because the gates are down, doesn't mean the work should be any less professional.

Other options: Smaller indie presses, hybrid presses

There are a number of very fine literary publishing houses who put out excellent books; some even garner major awards, as did Paul Harding's *Tinkers*, which won the Pulitzer in 2010. These houses don't pay advances—or if they do, they're very small—but it's still a major accomplishment to publish through one and a great boost to your career. In fact, some industry insiders have observed that as traditional "big five" publishing becomes increasingly sales- and blockbuster-driven, those publishers look to smaller independent publishers as "farm teams," where authors can prove themselves before one of the bigger houses risks a large sum of money on them. This strikes me as gross exploitation of the independents, but nonetheless, independent publishers serve an important role—they tolerate risk and experimentation and are in a better position to nurture writers in the early stages of their careers. *Poets and Writers* magazine online features an extensive database of independent publishers searchable by genre that provides an excellent glimpse into what is published by these presses as well as the kinds of work each press is looking for. You can also find some presses through general online searches and, due to the growth of digital publishing, more publishers are appearing on the landscape all the time. Again, just as in submitting to a literary journal or magazine, it's important to research the general character of the press and what they publish though (now easily done on the Web) before you send a query.

As you might expect, with the tectonic digital shifts happening in publishing, some new models have arisen that straddle the line between traditional and self-publishing. Although each press is going to be a little different, these hybrid presses tend to offer lower or no advances in return for higher royalties and varying editing and promotional models. Some of them have turned into highly successful ventures (the UK's Bookouture, an ebookseller recently acquired by Hachette UK, is one) while others have fizzled. But each is certainly worth a look as you search out the right place for your book.

Finally, just as when you searched for an agent, it's no less important here to make sure you give each publisher a thorough vetting through the Preditors and Editors and Absolute Write water cooler, and remember that if an opportunity seems too good to be true, it probably is. Are you a relatively unknown, unpracticed writer who is suddenly being approached by a "publisher" who wants to print your book for an editing and publishing fee that runs into several thousand dollars? When you look up said publisher on Google or on Amazon, do you find a long list of out-of-print books or books whose covers look like they were collaboratively produced by a kindergarten class? Are people complaining about being ripped off by them on the Internet? These are sure signs that you should proceed no further.

Finally, don't give up!

While book publishing can seem a capricious, almost arbitrary, business, that may be, in part, its beauty. You don't have to take failure in this realm entirely personally. If you believe in something you've written, truly believe in it, and if you've received encouraging responses to the work as a whole, there's no reason you shouldn't keep trying to bring it to readers. Besides, if you give up too soon, you'll never know if you were on the verge of finding your champion. The publishing world is full of stories of writers who succeeded after their umpteenth rejection—from Margaret Mitchell to Stephen King from Nabokov to J. K. Rowling. The next one really could be you—but only if you keep going.

12

Before you go: Why we do this

Before we part, let me remind you once more, you don't have to be cool to be a writer. You do not have to be anointed. And I am living proof. For evidence, look no further than the following two lists: "Cool" Things I Have Never Done and Very Uncool Things I *Have* Done. I think you will find them quite convincing, and comforting in their own way.

"Cool" Things I Have Never Done

1   Played in a band.

2   Hard drugs.

3   Hard liquor.

4   Gotten a tattoo or a body piercing.

5   Played poker. With other writers. (My youngest tried to teach me Texas Hold'em a few times when he was a kid but I could never figure it out. It didn't help that he had a tendency to make up his own rules when he started to lose.)

6   Smoked a cigar. Preferably while playing poker.

Very Uncool Things I *Have* Done

1 Got married at the age of 26.

2 Stayed married.

3 Had two kids. (One child is almost acceptable in the literary arts. Almost. However, unless you're Nicole Krauss, Julianna Baggott, Beth Ann Fennelly, or another equally talented and hip female writer, more than one is definitely not.)

4 Swooned over the complete works of Nat King Cole, B. J. Thomas, and Johnny Mathis throughout my teens and twenties, when all the cool people were following Joy Division and The Smiths. You might argue that this swooning is balanced out by my equal devotion to Peter Gabriel, Paul Simon, and Chicago, but in the end, it's a wash. My musical tastes embarrass even me. I have nothing to say for them.

5 Written, a lot, about the fact that creative writing could be taught better. Should be taught better. However, some writers who teach think it's very uncool to act as if you actually care about teaching. I think those writers should find other jobs.

6 Worn Crocs enthusiastically (go ahead, cringe now) during a brief period of temporary fashion insanity when I was at a total loss about my sky-high arches. I still look forward to the *Footsmart* catalog every month (my feet are a mess, honestly) but even I have come to my senses about Crocs.

7 Taken my family to Disney World. Granted, it was for a professional conference—my husband and I would never have gone to that kind of expense on our own. Rather, we prefer to spend equally exorbitant amounts of money schlepping our kids around Europe so that they can fulfill their dreams of

owning Yu-Gi-Oh! cards in every language. (This proclivity is almost cool—but it's hardly enough to make up for everything else.)

8   Driven a minivan, which I loved, for almost ten years. In fact, I would still be driving said minivan if it wasn't for a certain meth head who rear-ended me one day then got on his hands and knees and begged me not to call the police because he was trying to "get straight with the Lord." I tell you, I will miss that van till the end of my days. The very end. *That*, dear reader, is how unhip I am.

At this point, if you're thinking, "Good Lord, even *I'm* not that uncool," I've made my point. But seriously, I've spent most of this book driving home the fact that the writer's life isn't just for a select few, but something available to anyone with the will to pursue it because, as you've discovered if you've read to this point, such a life, while it has its compensations, is not easy. I've given you strategies for realizing some of the possible rewards of this life, especially publishing and connecting with readers, joining the writing community, supporting yourself, furthering your education, and venturing into the world of book publishing. But ultimately, while some of these rewards will help keep you going as a writer, they are not the reasons why we do this.

We write because we must, because we have something to say. Because we are writing geeks. We write because we are the kinds of people who have to get ideas, stories out of our heads and onto the page—or in whatever format the words take. This is what makes us writers. No one has the right to tell you differently.

It's possible that you might decide you didn't have that much to say after all, that the same energies you poured into writing were even better realized as a non-profit director, a landscape designer, a full-time parent. It's possible that you might decide this and still return to your writing in a few years when your life seems more balanced or when the well of words is overflowing again. Depending on what you expect from it (remembering my lawyer story from Chapter 1), writing isn't an all-or-nothing proposition. You can change your mind about it. The most important thing about a writing life, however, is that it is *your* choice. No one else gets to make it for you. That means you have to be especially well fortified against those who want to influence your decision, because they will try to. Over and over and over.

As I also said in Chapter 1, because of our society's whole screwed-up idea of the incompatibility of financial success and art, there will be people in your life who will continuously try, overtly and subtly, to divert you from your writing and you need to be ready for this. They will scoff at the time you take to write, they will ask things like, "what have you published lately? Is it anything I've read? Are you making it pay?" Whether they are simply ignorant, insensitive, tone-deaf, or someone who knows how to get under your skin, they will probably belittle your work or your ambition. If they feel they have any say in your life (although, if you are self-supporting, they don't—no one really does) they may even tell you flat out not to write, to give up on that crazy little dream, even if you are doing it on the side and it's hurting no one.

You must resist. And in resisting, it helps to understand the reason why you experience this, why the demeaning of writers and artists is so commonplace in our society as to be a cliché. It's endemic. It's also a cycle. Every single person who demeans your writing dreams had a dream once, to pursue their own creativity, whether through music, writing, drawing, something. And at a certain point in their growing up, someone, possibly multiple someones, mocked them for it or told them to stop and so they did. Over time, they became bitter and the belief took hold that if they could not express themselves in art, if they could not follow their dreams of living lives with some creative component, no one else should either. This is their motivation, whether conscious or not, in stopping *you*.

If they weren't anointed, ain't no one going to be anointed. They have skin in the game. This is why they are doing this to you.

Listen to me. You only get one life. I repeat.

You only get one life.

You do not get one life to live for yourself and another to make your parents or your partner or your best friend happy or at least keep them quiet. You only get the one and once it's gone, it's gone. If the process of weaving words together satisfies you in ways nothing else does, because you are a writing geek, *you must do it*. You must do it or you risk exuding the same bitterness, the same resentment of those who tried to stop you.

You know exactly what I'm talking about.

Like I said, it won't be easy. Despite receiving moral and material support for which I'm grateful, there have also been many, many times in my life when I simply had to turn a deaf ear to people who did not think I could succeed, who pressed me to choose something else, to become a lawyer, a pediatrician, an elementary-school teacher, the list goes on … I was polite, but steadfast, in my refusal to consider anything else, focusing instead on how to support myself and my family while staying true to my goals. That is what this book is about. My husband did the same thing—but how he did that is his own story to tell. This is mine.

There were many times when I could have given up, when it got really hard. I've told you about it—I didn't have as much money as some of my friends who were out working when I was still in graduate school, learning to write and living in rented rooms on rice and beans. I was the victim of an assault and an attempted kidnapping in the first year of my MFA program and many people expected me to turn tail then. What, they wondered was a twenty-two-year-old woman doing in 1990s Washington, D.C., a thousand miles from home? But I stayed. Leaving was not an option. Studying with the writers in that program—Richard Bausch, Susan Shreve, and Alan Cheuse—was critical to my development as a writer and I knew it: There would be no turning back.

Every step since then has just made me more determined, even if I had to sacrifice sleep, recreation, and disposable income to be true to that twenty-two-year-old and to help you be true to you. Because I knew that I had been given just as much. And so have you. Being fed, being sated, by this process, by the process of creating or preserving something of this life with language is a true gift, one that the universe does not bestow upon everyone but that it has seen fit to bestow upon you. It matters far more that you simply use it than whether or how much you publish or who you know or whether anyone else cares if you ever write another word.

Accept the gift. Treasure it. It is sacred. And it is all yours.

Appendix

Resources for Writers

Books to Inspire

I've read and taught dozens of writing life books. These are the best.

Black, Robin *Crash Course: Essays From Where Writing and Life Collide*. Indianapolis: Engine Books, 2016.

Cameron, Julia *The Right to Write: An Invitation and Initiation into the Writing Life*. New York: Tarcher: 1999.

Gilbert, Elizabeth *Big Magic: Creative Living Beyond Fear*. New York: Riverhead, 2015.

Lerner, Betsey *The Forest for the Trees: An Editor's Advice to Writers*. 2nd Edition New York, Riverhead, 2010.

Loyd, Carol *Creating a Life Worth Living*. New York: Perennial, 1997.

Katz, Cristina *Writer Mama: How to Build a Writing Career Alongside Your Kids*. Cinncinati: Writer's Digest, 2007.

Kleon, Austin *Steal Like an Artist: 10 Things Nobody Told You About Being Creative*. New York: Workman, 2012.

Kooser, Ted and Steve Cox. *Writing Brave and Free: Encouraging Words for People Who Want to Start Writing*. Lincoln, NE: Bison, 2006.

Lamott, Ann *Bird By Bird: Some Instructions on Writing and Life*. New York: Anchor, 1995.

Moore, Dinty W. *The Mindful Writer: Noble Truths and the Writing Life*. New York: Simon & Schuster: 2016.

Sellers, Heather *Page After Page: Discover the Confidence & Passion You Need to Start Writing & Keep Writing (No Matter What!)*. Cinncinati: Writer's Digest, 2009.

Stafford, Kim. *The Muses Among Us: Eloquent Listening and Other Pleasures of the Writer's Craft*. Athens, GA: University of Georgia P, 2003.

Books About the Field

Beevas, Dara and Amy Quale *Social Media Secrets for Authors: A Beginner's Guide to Blogging, Twitter, Facebook, and Goodreads.* Minneapolis: WiseInk, 2013.

Dweck, Carol S. *Mindset: The New Psychology of Success.* New York: Random House, 2006.

Friedman, Jane *Publishing 101: A First-Time Author's Guide to Getting Published, Marketing and Promoting Your Book, and Building a Successful Career.* Charlottesville, VA: MBA Press, 2014.

Houghton, Robin *Blogging for Writers: How Authors and Writers Build Successful Blogs.* Cinncinati: Writer's Digest Books, 2014.

Kealey, Tom *The Creative Writing MFA Handbook: A Guide for Prospective Students.* London: Bloomsbury Academic, 2008.

May, Lori *The Low Residency MFA Handbook: A Guide for Prospective Creative Writing Students.* London: Bloomsbury Academic, 2011.

May, Lori *The Write Crowd: Literary Citizenship and the Writing Life.* London: Bloomsbury Academic, 2014.

Sambuchino, Chuck *Create Your Writer Platform: The Key to Building an Audience, Selling More Books, and Finding Success as an Author.* Cinncinati, Writer's Digest Books, 2012.

Zantrop, Ashley C. Anderson et al *Now What? The Creative Writer's Guide to Success After the MFA.* Fairfield, CT: Fairfield UP, 2014.

Time Management Resources

Glei, Jocelyn, K. *Manage Your Day-To-Day: Build Your Routine, Find Your Focus, and Sharpen Your Creative Mind.* New York: 99u, 2013.

Self Control App. This app allows you to block selective social media sites for certain amounts of time. I don't know what Id do without it. selfcontrolapp.com

Resources for Inspiration

Katz, Christina *The Writer's Workout: 366 Tips, Tasks, & Techniques From Your Writing Career Coach.* Cinncinati: Writer's Digest Books, 2011.

Daily tips on creative writing from the author of *Writer Mama.*

Painter, Pamela and Ann Bernays *What If: Writing Exercises for Fiction Writers.* New York: Pearson, 2009.

Wood, Monica *The Pocket Muse*. Cinncinati: Writer's Digest Books, 2004.
The *Now Write* Book Series. New York: Tarcher.

Writing Exercises Site: http://writingexercises.co. uk/index.php

For such a boring name, there are a host of interesting randomized inspirations on this site, such as the random image generator and the random first line generator.

Writing Challenges

National Novel Writing Month The original writing challenge. nanowrimo.com
National Poem Writing Month http://www.napowrimo.net
National Nonfiction Writing Month http://writenonfictionnow.com/about-write-nonfiction-in-november/
AcWriMo http://www.phd2published.com/acwri-2/acbowrimo/about/
    Month-long writing event for academics.
Storyaday http://storyaday.org
Yeahwrite http://yeahwrite.me Weekly writing challenges

Books and Publishing News and Resources

Book Reviews

New York Times Book Review http://www.nytimes.com/section/books/review
Los Angeles Times Book Review http://www.latimes.com/books/
Rain Taxi www.raintaxi.com
Rain Taxi promotes literary culture by reviewing literary books.
Women's Review of Books http://www.wcwonline.org/Women-s-Review-of-Books/womens-review-of-books
The New York Review of Books http://www.nybooks.com
The London Review of Books http://www.lrb.co.uk
Another semi-monthly review of books and ideas with a European bent.

Literary News and Writing Communities

Litreactor http://litreactor.com
SheWrites http://www.shewrites.com

Vibrant writing community for promoting women writers.
Lithub http://lithub.com
Fictionaut http://fictionaut.com/blog
Writer Unboxed http://writerunboxed.com
Figment http://figment.com
TeenInk (for the younger crowd) http://www.teenink.com
Wattpad https://www.wattpad.com

Publishing News

Publisher's Weekly http://www.publishersweekly.com
Writer Beware http://www.sfwa.org/other-resources/for-authors/writer-beware/
Jane Friedman http://janefriedman.com/blog/
Preditors and Editors http://pred-ed.com
Chuck Wendig http://terribleminds.com/ramble/blog/
Poet's and Writer's http://www.pw.org
AWP (Association of Writer's and Writing Programs) http://awpwriter.org

Submission Resources

Newpages http://www.newpages.com
Duotrope https://duotrope.com
Poet's and Writer's Classifieds http://www.pw.org/classifieds
Literary Mama Calls for Submissions http://www.literarymama.com/blog
Creative Writing Opportunities List https://beta.groups.yahoo.com/neo/groups/
    CRWROPPS-B/info
The Practicing Writer http://www.erikadreifus.com/newsletter/current/

Cover Letters

http://thereviewreview.net/publishing-tips/your-perfect-cover-letter

Query Letters

https://janefriedman.com/query-letters/

Book Synopses

http://www.publishingcrawl.com/2012/04/17/how-to-write-a-1-page-synopsis/

Further Education

MFA Resources

The following articles will be helpful to those seeking further education, especially the MFA:

Poet's and Writer's MFA database and articles http://www.pw.org/mfa
AWP Guide to Writing Programs https://www.awpwriter.org/guide/overview
The MFA Blog http://creative-writing-mfa-handbook.blogspot.com
(Only current to 2014 but the site has some good information)
The MFA Draft https://www.facebook.com/groups/638437382879812/

Writer's Conferences

If you're interested in attending writing conferences or residencies, these sites will help you narrow your search.

18 Writer's Conferences Every Writer Should Attend http://thejohnfox.com/
    2016/07/writing-conferences-conventions-workshops/
Poet's and Writer's Conferences and Residencies Database http://www.pw.org/
    conferences_and_residencies

Writing Residencies

http://post-mfa.tumblr.com/residencies
http://www.artistcommunities.org/what-we-do

Careers in Editing and Publishing

Columbia Publishing Course (formerly the Radcliffe Publishing Course, one of the major courses for book publishing) https://journalism.columbia.edu/columbia publishing-course

Denver Publishing Institute http://www.du.edu/publishinginstitute/
NYU Summer Publishing Institute http://www.scps.nyu.edu/academics/
    departments/publishing/academic-offerings/summer-publishing-institute.
    html
Bookjobs Clearinghouse site for careers in publishing. http://www.bookjobs.com

Finding an Agent

Agent Query Agentquery.com
Query Tracker Querytracker.net
Chuck Sambuchino's Guide to Literary Agents Blog http://www.writersdigest.com/
    editor-blogs/guide-to-literary-agents

Independent and Small Publishers

Small Presses Database http://www.pw.org/small_presses

Index